A YEAR OF THE LORD

A YEAR OF THE LORD

Herbert O'Driscoll

*Reflections of Christian faith from the Advent of the Christ Child
to the Reign of Christ as King*

**Anglican Book Centre
Toronto, Canada**

1986
Anglican Book Centre
600 Jarvis Street
Toronto, Ontario
Canada M4Y 2J6

Typesetting by Jay Tee Graphics Ltd.
Printed and bound in Canada

Canadian Cataloguing in Publication Data

O'Driscoll, Herbert, 1928-
  A year of the Lord

ISBN 0-919891-54-3

1. Church year meditations. 2. Bible -
Meditations. 3. Meditations. I. Title.

BV30.037 1986   242'.3   C86-094824-2

Morehouse-Barlow Co., Inc.
78 Danbury Road
Wilton, Connecticut 06897

Library of Congress Cataloging-in-Publication Data

O'Driscoll, Herbert
  A year of the Lord.

1. Church year sermons. 2. Sermons, American.
3. Episcopal Church — Sermons. 4. Anglican Church of
Canada — Sermons. 5. Sermons, English — Canada. I. Title.

BX5937.045Y43 1986   252'.6   86-23835

ISBN 0-8192-1400-0

for Lorraine Melchior, Fred Valentine, Glenn Curtis, Forbes Newman, Eve Templeton, and Bob Griffiths, churchwardens and priest colleague while these pages were being written, hereafter friends; and for the worshipping community of Christ Church, Elbow Park, among whom one has the privilege of ministry

Contents

Preface

In many Christian churches there is a quiet and largely un-heralded revolution going on in the use of the Bible. The focus of this activity is called the Common Lectionary. The term *common* is to some extent a misnomer because, while this wider selection of scriptures is now used by many traditions, each one has made some adaptations in the selection of passages. To that extent no absolutely common lectionary exists.

However, what is common far outweighs the minor differences. The result is that, on any given Sunday morning, millions of Christians are for the first time hearing the same three passages of scripture, one from the Old Testament and two from the New Testament (indeed, two from the Old Testament if we include the regular use of the psalms). That use of scripture is taking those millions of Christians on a three-year journey through the Bible, and it is allowing them to experience a deep scriptural unity which cannot but affect the future of Christian communal worship, teaching, and practice.

The traditions which now use this selection of scripture are already finding that it is giving to preaching a new emphasis and a new discipline. In many cases it is leading to the return of the holy eucharist, or holy communion, or the mass, as the main act of the worshipping community on Sunday morning. This use of scripture is strongly encouraging the preacher to link together scriptures and homily or sermon. While the new lectionary gives ample opportunity to combine the themes of scripture, especially those of the Old Testament and gospel readings, it does not demand that linkages always be made. It is quite allowable for the preacher to take any one of the readings and develop whatever themes he or she finds emerging from it.

There is another aspect of contemporary Christian experience affecting Christian preaching. It is the realization that for many reasons much of the Christian story has been forgotten or is remembered only in a very fragmented way. To say that many are aware of Bible stories (and even these are often retained only vaguely) is not to say that they are aware of the story of the Bible. To the degree that this is acknowledged, there is a marked return to preaching that does not assume in the listener a knowledge of the incident or the event being spoken about. This has the effect of making much contemporary preaching strongly narrative. However, it is being discovered that the story can be so powerful in itself that it needs far less explanation and interpretation than formerly thought. If we wish any confirmation of this, we have only to look at the way in which our Lord himself communicated!

I mention these elements because they will be seen in these homilies.

The sequence in which I have written is primarily that of the liturgical or church year, commencing at Advent and ending at the Reign of Christ, but there is some adaptation to the natural sequence in the life of our Lord (for example, the Annunciation). I have not kept to the scriptures of any particular year of the three-year cycle. Sometimes I have concentrated on one passage rather than making any links between it and the others of the day. When I have done so, that passage will always be common to the lectionaries of both the Canadian Anglican and American Episcopal traditions, and will be common to almost all other uses of the Common Lectionary. Sometimes, when there have been slight differences between the above two streams (mainly in the selections of the Old Testament), I have included both selections and have woven them together. The simple and beautiful reality which Christians have long known is that scripture is, by its very nature, a seamless robe of endlessly interwoven meanings. It is that profound reality, at present being discovered by many, which is making the use of the Common Lectionary a new and exciting experience in Christian worship.

The College of Preachers in Washington, D.C., where these lines of preface were written, has been committed to furthering the excellence of preaching in and beyond the Anglican communion. In recent years it has included in its program regular conferences on the lections of each of the three years in the lectionary cycle. Those conferences continue, among many others, to deal with all aspects of homilizing.

Christ Church
Elbow Park
Calgary
Alberta
Pentecost 1986

Acknowledgements

My sincere thanks to Erin Sellers for putting these pages on the word processor, ably assisted by Lois Cutler; to Sue Johnsen, my secretary, for her constant assistance in arranging, typing, and making copies; and to Mark Perrin with whose help and encouragement I am beginning, very tentatively, my own encounter with the world of word processing.

Advent

A Season of Expectation

In those days and at that time I will cause a righteous Branch to spring forth for David; and he shall execute justice and righteousness in the land. Jeremiah 23:5

"And there will be signs in sun and moon and stars, and upon the earth distress of nations in perplexity at the roaring of the sea and the waves, men fainting with fear and with foreboding of what is coming on the world; for the powers of the heavens will be shaken. And then they will see the Son of man coming in a cloud with power and great glory. Now when these things begin to take place, look up and raise your heads, because your redemption is drawing near." Luke 21:25–28

For now we live, if you stand fast in the Lord. 1 Thessalonians 3:8

In the year 1793 on an August afternoon in the great prison of the Bastille in Paris, a man was desperately trying to finish a book. He had a good idea that he would die very soon. He was correct. He was executed within twenty-four hours. His name was the Marquis de Condorcet. Although once very nearly forgotten, he is now recognized in this decade as one of the modern world's great futurists. The book he was writing was *The Progress of the Human Mind*. In that book de Condorcet forms a picture of a future world, and his predictions are amazingly prescient. He foresaw what we would call the feminist movement. He foresaw women's suffrage, universal education, the sexual revolution, the insurance industry, even genetic engineering.

As the twentieth century moves to an end, we are fascinated with the subject of the future. It is the subject of conferences. Foundations give money for endless symposiums about it. Men and women make careers out of "futurizing." Corporations spend vast sums commissioning reports on the future. We are

not the first age to do this. A concern with the future occurs particularly in periods of great change and turmoil. A universal
uncertainty creates a universal anxiety and curiosity about the
future. Marshall McLuhan once said that there come times when
the pain of the present is so great that people try to go into the
future.

Look for a moment at the book we know as the Bible. It is possible to say that the whole sequence of it centres around and moves
towards two great scenarios of the future. The scriptures of
Judaism, what Christians call the Old Testament, point toward
a vision of the future. It is usually referred to as the Day of the
Lord. The vision, or rather the various images and visions, all
try to picture a world where the rule of God is fully established
and where God's will and humanity's will have become one.
There are many versions of it, and Jeremiah's images in the
passage above are among the many.

For Isaiah, the coming of the rule of God is seen as a holy mountain where ''the lion shall lie down with the lamb,'' where things
that seem irreconcilable will be reconciled. It is a vision of *shalom*.

For the prophet Amos, the Day of the Lord is looked to as a
time when ''justice shall flow down like many waters.''

The prophet Joel emphasizes a darker aspect. He sees the
coming of God primarily as a terrible judgement. He remembers
the sudden sky-darkening plagues of locusts on the land and
points to that as a terrible image of divine judgment.

Malachi's images of the Day of the Lord are particularly powerful because they are the very final verses of the Old Testament.

> For behold, the day comes, burning like an oven, when all the
> arrogant and all evildoers will be stubble; the day that comes
> shall burn them up, says the Lord of hosts, so that it will leave
> them neither root nor branch. But for you who fear my name
> the sun of righteousness shall rise, with healing in its wings.
> You shall go forth leaping like calves from the stall. And you
> shall tread down the wicked, for they will be ashes under the
> soles of your feet, on the day when I act, says the Lord of hosts.

Before we examine the words of Jeremiah, let's remember that
we are meeting this prophet in the season of Advent. Maybe it
would help to think for a few moments about Advent.

First of all, it is a season. That may seem very obvious, but I mention it for a particular reason. Each of the seasons, whether it be Advent (before Christmas) or Epiphany (after Christmas) or Lent (before our Lord's passion) or Easter (after the actual day itself), uses a rich collection of scriptures, taken from both testaments, the psalms, and sometimes the Apocrypha. Together they form a kind of orchestra playing a vast and complex symphony of faith, the theme of which is both simple enough for a child's hearing while being utterly profound and majestic in meaning.

At the heart of the Christian faith are certain great mysteries. One of these is the birth of Mary's child, the event we have called the Incarnation, the coming of God in human flesh. This basic element of faith can never be exhausted as a source of reflection. Christians, knowing that, have placed the event, focused in one day, within a longer season, so that some of its different images and innumerable meanings may be brought to mind.

Advent is a season of expectation. The word itself means that. We expect something to come. What is that something? It is the growing expectation of the birth of our Lord Jesus Christ. But what exactly do we mean by such language. Obviously we are not claiming that in a physical sense Mary again gives birth in some geographical twentieth-century Bethlehem. So then, what do we mean? Such a question is reasonable in an age when Christians need to commend their faith to a society which has both lost faith and yet longs for faith. It is difficult to find words for what we believe. We needn't be worried about that. Explanation and mystery are uneasy companions.

Advent is a season when Christians prepare to recall something that happened long ago. But why go on recalling a memory? Because this particular memory is of something or someone who by entering past time changed the meaning of time and gave us a new way of thinking about the future. This memory on which Christian faith is founded (in this season the birth of Jesus Christ) creates for us the hope of a future time when what we saw come true in him (ultimate love and the capacity to conquer death) is what we will see come true for the whole creation. That is the mystery and the hope, the dream if you will, which the whole season of Advent expresses. Its scriptures, its psalms, its hymns, its homilies or sermons are all trying to express at least a facet of this hope.

With that in mind we look at the words we have of Jeremiah. Like all the prophets of the Bible, Jeremiah has the difficult task of telling his contemporaries the truth about themselves. But, again like the other prophets, Jeremiah feels called by God to give his listeners the kind of hope which will motivate them to make a commitment to the future. In other words, he must give them a dream, an expectation, an Advent. What does he choose to give them as a hope? He envisions a society where there will be righteousness, justice, and security. He offers this, not as a dream which pacifies people into wishful hoping but as a vision which galvanizes them into action.

That trio of righteousness, justice, and security is an ''advent'' or expectation that still motivates millions of men and women in today's world. For some it is a dream of peace, of international detente. For some it is a hope of a recovery of the spiritual elements of life in our society, or an improvement in the overall quality of life. For some it is seen as a freedom from hunger and grinding poverty or repressive political and economic regimes.

The moment we realize that the whole point of possessing a hope or an advent is to motivate action, we realize how necessary it is for any age or any society, including our own, to possess such an advent. What can it mean then for our society to look for ''the birth of the Christ child''?

On a personal level, expecting the Christ child means that I offer myself, my own inner life, as the place of Christ's new birth. I offer myself as today's manger in which he can come again and be laid. I offer my intentions and motivations as the clothes which will swaddle him. The elemental things of my life — my appetites, my fears, my emotions — can be the shepherds who kneel before him. The intellectual things of my life — my wonderings, my questions, my theories — can be the magi or wise men who acknowledge him as King.

Suppose that such images succeed in grasping what I as a Christian might hope for and resolve to seek in Advent. What effect might such hopes, such images, have on my life? It seems to me that they give me the hope of the possibility of new birth in me, a new birth which seeks to live out, even in an unworthy way, what I see and know to be of Christ. I try to allow the memory of Jesus' birth to open me to the experience of the living Christ in the present, so that I may offer myself to bring about his will for the future.

With those thoughts in mind, we look at the passage from the gospel. Jesus is speaking to the disciples. He uses the images of an apocalyptic time. He describes, in those timeless images, an age of change, turmoil, fear, anxiety, natural catastrophe, social and political upheaval. The images are just as effective as a description of the age we live in. But when Jesus ends that terrible list, he says extraordinary things. He tells his disciples that, when such times come, they will see the Son of man coming. They should then lift up their heads because their redemption is near.

What do such statements mean? We need to do a great deal of wrestling with these words because they have become immensely significant to Christians in the late twentieth century. To some Christians they are perfectly obvious and need no explanation. They mean that this age we are in, to which Jesus' description can well apply, will soon end. Christ will come in judgement. This age will end and a new age will begin. In that age the "redeemed" will become part of the kingdom or reign of Christ.

Is there another way in which we can receive this passage, without in any way denying that the consummation of all human history lies in God's power and plan? I think there is. I think it is necessary to take the grace of this scripture and apply it to our age, even if we do not agree that it is the ending of human history. We may consider this an age of deep and vast change and turmoil and danger. There is ample evidence that it is! But there have been other such ages, through which God has demanded men and women live as transition to another age.

If that is true, then how can this scripture be grace to us today? I think we must look again at those statements of our Lord. He speaks to his disciples. You and I offer ourselves to be his contemporary disciples. He speaks of our age, describing its shadows. The climax is the image of the Son of man coming. He then tells us to lift up our heads because our redemption is near.

Is it possible to understand our Lord telling us that in an age such as ours we will recover the realization that there is a son and daughter relationship between us and God, and that this relationship is hidden in our humanity, half-forgotten and neglected, until apocalyptic times and conditions bring it to birth in us again? In other words, through adversity God forces us to face the conditions which our sinful human behaviour has brought about. In response, if we so choose, we can discover a reborn humanity that gives us the grace to take courage and offer our gifts to God for the building of the next chapter of his plan, for which Christ came into time and history.

To hear scripture say all this is not to deny it a more mysterious and final meaning. There will come a time of ultimate ending. There will come a time when the transition will be not from one age of ongoing human history to another but from this age to the new age. In that moment God, through Christ, will place the crown of his own purpose and will on creation.

Here, then, is an attempt to express some of the mystery of this season. Advent, meaning expectation, includes many levels of expectation. There is the expectation of the coming of the Christ child. That event comes to us in the loveliness, the art, the family reunions, the music of Christmas. However, there is also, for a Christian, the expectation of judgement on human history. That comes to us in the very real threats our world faces from the sum total of our choices and actions. Without the hope that we possess in the image of the holy birth, we can be overcome by the images of threat and danger. One is an image of light, the other of darkness. It is Saint John who reminds us that the light shines in the darkness and the darkness does not overcome it.

Advent

A Voice in the Wilderness

In the fifteenth year of the reign of Tiberius Caesar, Pontius Pilate being governor of Judea, and Herod being tetrarch of Galilee, and his brother Philip tetrarch of the region of Ituraea and Trachonitis, and Lysanias tetrarch of Abilene, in the high-priesthood of Annas and Caiaphas, the word of God came to John the son of Zechariah in the wilderness; and he went into all the region about the Jordan, preaching a baptism of repentance for the forgiveness of sins. As it is written in the book of the words of Isaiah the prophet,

"The voice of one crying in the wilderness:
Prepare the way of the Lord,
make his paths straight.
Every valley shall be filled,
and every mountain and hill shall be brought low,
and the crooked shall be made straight,
and the rough ways shall be made smooth;
and all flesh shall see the salvation of God."

He said therefore to the multitudes that came out to be baptized by him, "You brood of vipers! Who warned you to flee from the wrath to come? Bear fruits that befit repentance, and do not begin to say to yourselves, 'We have Abraham as our father'; for I tell you, God is able from these stones to raise up children to Abraham. Even now the axe is laid to the root of the trees; every tree therefore that does not bear good fruit is cut down and thrown into the fire." Luke 3:1–9

Notice how totally political and precise that passage of the gospel is. It says that when Augustus ruled the empire as Caesar, when Herod ruled the local area, when Caiaphas was high priest, a certain man spoke about the future in a way that was vivid and electrifying. He simply could not be ignored. He drew crowds. He made people profoundly thoughtful. He made them consider their life-styles. He even made some change their lives.

That man's name was John Bar Zachariah. History calls him John the Baptist. What he said can be expressed very succinctly. He was convinced that his generation was living through a very significant moment of history, and that it was going to exact all their moral, political, and social fibre to do so. They were going to be held accountable for their decisions, both personal and corporate. He climaxed his remarks by saying that if that supreme challenge was met, if deep changes were brought about in the society, then a future was possible where human life could be lived with fulfilment, creativity, and hope, both personally and politically.

John did not, of course, use that kind of language. He spoke in the imagery of his time. He quoted a great poet whose words would be perfectly familiar to every one of his listeners — the prophet Isaiah.

Every valley will be exalted.
The crooked shall be made straight.
Rough ways shall be made smooth,
and all flesh shall see the salvation of God.

All that happened long ago. But the question we always have to ask about the Bible is whether the *content* of what happened is also past. Consider something. Not yet a decade ago, when certain people were in office in this country, when a certain man or woman was your political representative, when a certain man was bishop in your church, something important and rather chilling was said about the future. It was said in the form of a report called *Global 2000*. It told us that, if certain patterns of contemporary life were to continue as they are now to the end of this millenium, irreparable damage will have been done to the fragile ecosystem which envelops this planet, thereby putting in danger the equally fragile social and political fabric of life. The grim thesis was buttressed by layer upon layer of implacable calculation.

Here then are two statements. One is made by a man two thousand years ago in a tiny society, the other is brought on to the world stage by banks of whirring computers. They use two kinds of language to say much the same thing. They both insist that humanity is under judgement. The first, the statement of the biblical prophet, says that humanity is accountable to a reality beyond itself. The report *Global 2000* probably would have defined that reality as the laws of nature or the universe. John the Baptist defined it with incisive simplicity. He named it God.

All of us alive today are moving through a profoundly significant moment of time. It is a moment from which, as always, different roads run into the future. One is a highway of immense, though by no means effortless, possibility. The other road leads to almost inexpressible threat and tragedy. Each of these exists as a potential "advent."

Advent is the name of this season of sacred time. It means simply a "coming" or an "expectation." We can, if we wish, dismiss Advent as merely a religious concept. We can say it means nothing more than the name of the season when certain people who have chosen a certain religion celebrate the expectation of the birth of a long-ago child. If we did that, we would be missing something crucial. At its deepest level the Advent season asks a question which is never easy to answer. It is a question which in this decade we have particular difficulty facing. The question is something like this: In what terms do we think about the future? What do we really believe is coming? What is our expectation?

One kind of answer to that was recently given a great deal of publicity because of the person who reflected on it. At a recent national conference of authors, Ursula Le Guin, one of the most brilliant contemporary names in science fiction, said that she was appalled to realize that, when she recently published a new book about a future society on the west coast of this continent, she found that most readers presumed that the society had survived a nuclear war. Le Guin said she had come to realize, from chatting with many people, that most of us seem not to be able to envision a future without such a catastrophe.

The reason why our assumptions about the future are supremely important far beyond the bounds of any church or religion, important for the whole interwoven body politic of the world, is this: the categories in which men and women think about the future are themselves a factor in the formation of that future! For instance, as we have come to know very well in this century, when men and women in a society, particularly an oppressed or impoverished society, begin to consider the future in terms of "advent," an advent seen in terms of political liberation, that very attitude or dream energizes them to act powerfully and effectively towards the fulfilling of that dream. The categories in which we think of the future, the images of our advents, all play a part in our capacity to bring those futures about.

It is important for us to consider this because there may be something insidious and subtle happening in our society. First, let's look at what may seem no more than a popular and therefore deceptively harmless manifestation of it. Look along the racks of any drug store or airport bookshop. One-quarter of them usually contain horror stories. But look again. Of those horror stories about one-third, sometimes more, are stories of demonically possessed children. What does a child symbolize? A child is the symbol of things that are possible, of all that is not yet. A child is a symbol of the future. Considering this popular obsession with horrors and monstrosities involving children, are we really betraying our fear that the future has become essentially malignant?

Look for a moment at something other than popular paperbacks. A few years ago George Steiner of the faculty of Harvard, then visiting professor at Cambridge in England, was invited by the BBC to give the first Jacob Bronowski Memorial Lecture. Steiner titled his lecture "Has truth a future?" His thesis went something like this.

For many centuries Western society has been energized by an assumption deep in the heart of Judeo-Christian religion. It emerges from such biblical statements as "God saw that it (creation) was good" or that "a child is given unto us" (from Isaiah). It was also implicit in the belief that in Jesus Christ the divine had mysteriously entered in a new way into the human story. From this assumption, said Steiner, came the conviction that God or truth or the future or reality were essentially "for us," were essentially benevolent. From that kind of conviction came much of the energy and motivation of the West. This is not to deny that, because of the flawed nature of all human affairs, darker elements, such as arrogance and the pursuit of power, were also introduced into Western history.

That optimism, claims Steiner, has ended in our generation. We are now dangerously near believing, he suggests, that the future, whatever it be, is essentially malignant and fundamentally against us. It is not difficult to imagine the consequences of this, if it be true. If there is even partial truth in Steiner's thesis, it means that Western society could be moving from a dynamic and creative stance in history, not into a stance of greater responsibility and care in handling the awesome discoveries we have made, but into a stance of neurotic and fearful passivity.

You may feel like saying that, while all this may be interesting, it seems to have little to do with the good news of this Advent season. I suggest there is a very profound connection, a connection we may see when we consider what the emerging Christian faith was heard to communicate in that society in which it flourished during the first few centuries of its life. Let's listen to the heartbeat of the Mediterranean world around the year A.D. 275.

Within that very pluralistic society, poised on the edge of great transition, anticipating the end of a long-unchallenged empire, certain agonies were being wrestled with. The empire was still far from disintegrating, but the Roman mind was beginning to suspect that the course of history was somehow past high noon, that the shadows of the afternoon of Rome were beginning to lengthen. It was just possible that history was closing in, that there was not after all a broadening highway into the future but a ghastly cul-de-sac, where even the best of human hopes and efforts were doomed to crash against a terrible wall of futility and meaninglessness.

Into that society there sounded the voice of a new minority. It refused to believe that history was closed. When asked why, its voices said they had experienced among them a new quality of humanity, one named Jesus whom they entitled Christ. In him the divine had entered the human story in human form; therefore the highway of history, far from closing, was opening to immense future possibility.

There was another issue the new minority addressed. As the empire spread — northwest to the Grampian Hills in Britain, south to the edge of the Sahara, east to the bank of the Euphrates — two things seemed to be inevitably contaminating public life. To keep the legions marching, more and more of the energy and resources of the whole society had to be invested in defending far-flung borders. It was beginning to seem inevitable that a thin veneer of civilization could rest only on a growing base of militarism and the brutalization of life. Also, as the institutions of empire grew in extent and complexity, they lost the capacity to attract the energy of the finest lives and minds of Rome. A measure of cynicism and alienation towards institutions was developing. More and more citizens chose private rather than public life.

Into this faltering moment came again the voice of the new Christian minority. It refused to accept brutality, violence, and cynicism as the inevitable attributes of civilization. Christians claimed to have encountered in Jesus Christ a quality of existence whose primary characteristics, far from being violence and cynicism, were love and hope. Those characteristics, they claimed, had been proved unquenchable even by death itself.

We begin to see how, in a shadowed time of history and society, Christians dared to speak of light. In a time of seemingly narrowing historical options, they dared to speak of a broadening highway into the future. In a time of seemingly inevitable cultural death, they dared to speak of resurrection. In speaking of such things, have we been considering merely the long-ago or something timeless? Were the things that Christians then said dismissed as unrealistic, naïve, even pitable self-delusion? Of course they were, and by the best brains of the time! But that very naïvité proved to be the womb of a possible future, a future of which we are a part.

The next time you look at a paperback in the drugstore or airport and you look into the glistening melodramatized eyes of a demonically possessed child, you may recognize a symbol of contemporary loss of faith in the future. If you do, think of another child, a child lying in a manger. Think of a child in whose eyes shines what C.S. Lewis used to call "Deep Heaven." In that moment ask yourself, What commitment to the future is demanded of me precisely because I claim to be a follower of that child?

To that child, that "sacred infant all divine," to Jesus Christ, who is possessor and Lord of the future, be praise and glory.

The Coming of an Angel

Therefore the Lord himself will give you a sign. Behold, a young woman shall conceive and bear a son and shall call his name Immanuel. Isaiah 7:14

"Then I said, 'Lo, I have come to do thy will, O God,' as it is written of me in the roll of the book." Hebrews 10:7

And the angel said to her, "Do not be afraid, Mary, for you have found favour with God." Luke 1:30

Great art has given us unforgettable images of the moment when Mary became aware that she was to bear a child. On the canvas she sits calmly and regally. She acknowledges the winged messenger bowing in her presence. They gaze in rapt attention towards each other. They stand at an intersection between time and eternity, heaven and earth, humanity and God.

When I was a child growing up in the south of Ireland, there was a hired man on my grandfather's farm. His name was John Brennan. Very often in the summer evenings of my school holidays, he and I would chat. We would sit either on a long low stone in front of the farmhouse or on the shafts of the horse's cart. He told me many things which stayed in a child's mind. He told me one night, as the first stars began to appear in the still light sky, that, when the angel came to Mary and told her of her sublime vocation, there was a silence between the angel's news and Mary's response. John told me that in that silence all the suns and planets and stars ceased to move. When Mary replied, "Let it be to me according to your word," the universe once again began to move.

Art and story are woven to express the inexpressible. Because of course, this event is almost inexpressible. It is so profound and majestic, so full of cosmic significance that we have to turn to a certain kind of language to share it among us. For mystery there can only be the language of mystery.

Always in scripture angels are understood to be the messengers of God. We might find it helpful to reverse the statement and say that messages from God are our angels. With this understanding we realize that angels have visited us. Sometimes the message is of encouragement, sometimes of warning. Its mode of coming may be through any of the myriad means of communication in our culture. Letters, phone calls, casual conversations, periods of quiet reflection, a dream, arrow prayer, a passage of a book, an interval of music, a casual remark of a friend — all these things are messages borne on great wings, irrespective of the everyday disguise they have worn for us. We do not know what form Mary's angel took. We do not know what voice brought to her the realization of her vocation. We only know that she accepted it, and therefore the human future became utterly changed.

As with all scripture the past event speaks in the present, the past human experience has messages for our humanity. The angel addresses Mary and says, ''The Lord is with you,'' and scripture says that ''she was greatly troubled at the saying, and considered in her mind what sort of greeting this might be.'' There lies her deep wisdom. Messages within us — and we all experience them — have to be evaluated. The more intense and demanding they are, the more essential it is to do this. Messages within us can come from many different sources. They can be angelic and creative, or demonic and destructive. We do well if we are troubled or concerned when something deeply directive wells up within us and we feel called to specific action. We are wise if we examine very carefully ''what sort of greeting this might be.''

Such is Mary's concern that she feels actual fear. That is natural, totally human. As with everything else in our humanity, fear has a legitimate role. Fear acts as warning. It can give us time for consideration. Fear can clear our vision to see false notes in a possibility, to see traps, to realize that we are attracted to something that is essentially unwise and for our harm.

On the other hand, fear beyond a certain point can prevent action. It can keep us on the edge of possible action. At worst it can immobilize. Sometimes fear has its hold over us because of our own self-identity and self-image. We do not believe in our own abilities. We do not believe that others believe in us. It is significant that the message to Mary tells her that she is believed in: she has "found favour with God." That sense of being believed in by God, being trusted and accepted as one fitted for a particular task, in itself provides the grace for Mary to say *yes*. While the vocation asked of her was immense, actually beyond human comprehension, what is true of Mary is to a degree true of our own lives. If we have a sense of being given a vocation for a certain task, we may realize that the task has been given because we possess the ability to carry it out. We have, in Luke's language, "found favour with God." That does not mean that we are morally superior in any way. It means that God has confidence that we, with grace, can carry out God's purpose.

In our other scripture it is significant that, as Isaiah tries to encourage Ahaz his king, he speaks of a young woman giving birth. It is possible that Isaiah is using the image of that birth to call forth in Ahaz the birth of courage and creative planning and action in the face of the great threats facing Israel. To this image of birth Isaiah adds the name of a child. He tells Ahaz that the newborn will be called "God is with us." That is what the name Emmanuel means. Isaiah seems determined to get Ahaz to realize that God is with him, that his abilities and gifts, in fact his total humanity, is being offered the companionship and support of God.

To Mary comes the realization that, should she accept this vocation, she will "conceive . . . and bear a son." But, of course, that is precisely the reality we experience if we accept life as vocation. A sense of vocation, a sense that life is a process of responding to the initiatives of God for us, has the result of making us give birth to that which otherwise remains dormant within us. A sense of being called by God releases seeds within us which emerge as plans, dreams, purposes, actions. They become, if you will, the children which God conceives in us for his purposes.

We follow the conversation between Mary and her messenger. She has abandoned fear. Reassurance has made that possible. Fear gives way to mystification. "How shall this be," she asks, "since I have no husband?" Again the question and the response contain a truth for our lives. We can reflect on that truth without in any way lessening the unique setting in which the words are first voiced.

Mary is puzzled that conception could be possible when the normal relationship for its occurrence does not yet exist for her. There is a sense in which we can see such a syndrome in our own lives. Very often our instinct is that certain things cannot be actualized without others to help, to interact with us, to give us direction, to provide ideas, to fertilize the life already in us (if we can use the image of procreation). But sometimes the messenger of God is trying to get us to see that we have all we need to respond to God. Within ourselves we possess the seed that can grow to become the vessel for God's use.

What fertilizes that inner seed? Listen to the message to Mary. The voice says, "The Holy Spirit will come upon you, and the power of the Most High will overshadow you." The same message is given to us in an infinite number of ways. There may be a sudden rush of feeling, a deepening of a sense of the presence of God, a consciousness of great change in one's life. In a moment of reflection, in a time of worship, in a moment of prayer, in an hour of solitude, while listening to a passage of scripture, while reading a book, while walking or driving, while sitting at one's desk — in all these circumstances and many more we encounter and are encountered by the mystery we call the Holy Spirit.

The messenger adds for Mary a piece of news. She is told of Elizabeth and another expectation of a child. Notice how Elizabeth's conception has in common with Mary's a total unexpectedness. In Elizabeth's case the unexpected factor is age. What does this moment in Luke's passage say to our lives? Why is it more than a past incident?

There is a kind of rule in life. Many have experienced it. It turns out in human experience that, if a new reality comes into your life, you begin to notice others for whom this has also happened. Because you were not aware of it previously, you were not aware of it in them. A man or woman may find a bland and uncommitted interest in religion becoming a living faith. This faith seeks ways to exercise a new commitment, to grow and mature and learn. Soon that man or woman discovers others who share such a quest. They may have known each other before. They may have been fellow students or colleagues in business life. But they have never encountered one another on the level of faith. Mary and Elizabeth have known each other for years, but now they begin to discover a whole dimension of each other they have never explored before, because it did not exist before!

One thing more the messenger adds. "With God nothing is impossible." Why is that reassurance added? Perhaps because there is something in Mary's face or stance that seems to ask, "Why me? Why ordinary me?" The ancient world had a tradition of great persons being regarded as gods. Rome particularly fostered this tradition. Such things were not in the mental universe of a young village woman. Yet her simplicity is chosen, her obscurity, her humility.

It is so with us. Others are called to special vocation with fanfare. We think of them as spiritual giants. The very word *vocation* has been isolated into a rarified meaning which makes it almost impossible, at least unlikely, to apply to ourselves. Our bland religious beliefs become alive in a new way? Impossible. Our careful measured commitments become total commitment? Impossible! Our carefully cordoned off religious interests suddenly spill over into everything we do? Impossible! All the while the messenger waits until our alarmed protestations pause for breath. Into the interval a voice says quietly, "With God nothing is impossible," and, if we are wise, we are silent.

We have been reflecting on an event called the Annunciation. In following the conversation of Mary and her messenger, we have concentrated on the vocation that Mary is offered. The messenger does not merely come to impose a task. Mary is not directed to obey. The message begins by stating a possibility. Only if Mary accepts her vocation can the possibility become actuality. That is true of each of our lives. God invites. God offers us life as vocation. In the letter to the Hebrew Christians, there is a point where the writer puts certain words into the mouth of Christ. "Then I said, Lo, I have come to do thy will." But that is true of every human being who is prepared to see his or her life in terms of vocation. I exist to do God's will. To say that does not mean that my will and my identity are eliminated. It means that the whole thrust of my life is an effort to align my will with the will of God. That is exactly the meaning of the words which Luke gives to our Lord's mother. She says, "Behold, I am the handmaid of the Lord,'' and in that simple self-offering she defines all Christian vocation.

There is one more deceptively simple statement. ''The angel,'' Luke states, ''departed from her.'' There are long periods of life when the angel departs from you and from me, long periods when there is no sense of being particularly called, no sense of being in any way given messages or addressed by God in any specific way. In such periods it may help to realize that, although the angel left Mary, the conceiving made possible by her acceptance had already begun.

It is true for us too. When there is no discernible sense of any messenger, it might be wise to think back to a time when there was indeed that sense, to realize that seeds were planted at a time we may have since forgotten and neglected. It may be that we are not aware of messengers to us simply because we already have within us, from a long-ago encounter, the seeds of a vocation which we have only to offer again to feel the life of God stirring within us. To realize that is to realize why these things are called good news.

A Woman and Her Child

How beautiful upon the mountains are the feet of him who brings good tidings, who publishes peace, who brings good tidings of good, who publishes salvation, who says to Zion, "Your God reigns." Isaiah 52:7

In many and various ways God spoke of old to our fathers by the prophets; but in these last days he has spoken to us by a Son, whom he appointed the heir of all things, through whom also he created the world. Hebrews 1:1–2

In the beginning was the Word, and the Word was with God, and the Word was God. He was in the beginning with God; all things were made through him, and without him was not anything made that was made. John 1:1–3

And suddenly there was with the angel a multitude of the heavenly host praising God and saying, "Glory to God in the highest, and on earth peace among men with whom he is pleased!" Luke 2:13–14

Why has this season such extraordinary and unrelenting power? What is it that affects our society in every aspect of its being? Hospitals empty to a great extent, shops are thronged, airports are jammed, radio stations, usually all seeking their own unique "sound," begin for a few hours to sound alike. Every television program on every channel, whatever its plot, will set that particular episode in the context of this season. Families will gather, if at all possible; organizations will take steps to care for people; gifts will be given; relationships will be nourished by cards, letters, telephone calls. Actually, there is no end to the ways in which life is affected in these fleeting hours we call Christmas.

Why? There are, of course, many reasons. Most of them we express from time to time according to mood. If we are feeling cynical, we say it is all the creation of a greedy commercial system. If we are feeling intellectual, we like to chat about ancient Roman holidays celebrating the winter solstice. Sometimes we throw Charles Dickens into the conversation, calling him the creator of Christmas as we know it. But the fact is that none of these elements on their own could achieve what happens in these few hours.

I remember once being in a major international airport on the afternoon of Christmas Day. There were very few people around. The lights shone, the machines worked away, the TV screens dispensed their depleted information, someone slowly mopped a spill in the stand-up snack area. It was a time of day when this huge place would normally have been thundering and pulsating with activity. I remember realizing the power which had effected this. I realized that the birth of a child two thousand years before had reached across time and quieted this vast place, indeed, had quieted the world. Oh yes, the symbols were very mixed. The plastic holly and ivy had come from the pagan woods of northern Europe; the stage coach on the neon-lit sign was certainly from the world of Dickens. But none of these things on their own, certainly not a half-forgotten Roman celebration of the winter solstice, could have effected this without the Child who lies at the heart of it all.

Christmas is the Child, not just any child. It is about a particular child born to a particular woman in a particular place at a particular time. It is about a child whom she named and to whom we must also give another name. This is of paramount importance if we are to realize what is at issue here. His mother named him Jesus. Each of us who comes to Christmas in our own way and in our own time must decide whether or not we wish to add the title Christ.

What do I believe happened at that birth? The only one of the four evangelists who struggles to express it is Luke. Mark doesn't mention it. Matthew does, but emphasizes the coming of the magi. John expresses the birth in cosmic terms. For him the event takes place at the heart of the universe. He does not deny that time and eternity may very well intersect at that moment in Bethlehem, but he never mentions the town. Only Luke grapples with the mystery, and it is obvious that even Luke is aware that no precise factual information will suffice. But he is at pains to get away from the type of story that begins, "Long ago and far away." This birth, he seems to be saying, may have timeless and universal significance, but it is as real, as specific as any other human event. So Luke is very precise. The administration in the country is defined. The place is most specific. The relationship of Mary and Joseph is described in very human terms of struggle, pain, misunderstanding. Everything is grounded in the real and the particular.

But even though Luke emphasizes the particular, he cannot be imprisoned in that world. Somehow there is a quality about this event which breaks out of space and time. So Luke turns to the devices and the images which his culture frequently used to try to communicate great significance hidden in a specific event. Heaven is the infinite extension of his stage; angels are the voices of the totality of creation in which the human order is only a part. And when Luke gives us the song of the angels, it bridges in one magnificent sentence planet and universe, earth and heaven, humanity and the higher creation, time and eternity. That is what the angelic song does. That is what our limited minds and voices are enabled to do when we say or sing, "Glory to God in the highest and on earth peace among men with whom he is pleased."

One has only to try to speak about the meaning of this mystery we call Christmas and one finds oneself forsaking ordinary language. I have mentioned how Luke had to branch out into the most exalted concepts he could think of. We see exactly the same thing when we look at today's epistle. We don't know who wrote this letter to the Hebrew Christians. What we do know (because it becomes obvious as we read) is that the writer had an immense gift for lyrical imaginative prose. Like Luke he decides that the only screen big enough to show us the significance of the birth of Jesus Christ is a screen as wide as the universe! He is searching for ultimate language and ultimate images because he wishes to point out that in this child we are presented with a new order of being, the ultimate order of being in whom, in a totally mysterious way, humanity and God interface and become one!

If that is true — and this truth is the heart of the Christian faith — then what other language can you or I or anyone else use? Even the most exalted language falls short. In twelve verses of his first chapter the writer to the Hebrews roams from one end of the universe to the other and from the formation of the earth to the present time, not to mention going beyond space and time into the biblical realm of angels! Listen to Isaiah, the most lyrical and vivid singer who ever lived.

I deliberately list these things because it is not an accident that they ring bells in our late twentieth-century consciousness. In fact, the way in which these lines of Isaiah can speak in today's context is an ideal way to realize the timelessness of the Bible.

Consider first why the early Christians very soon began to turn to Isaiah as they looked for ways to express what they believed about their Lord. When they looked at a passage such as this, they paralleled the long-ago imagining of freedom from exile and the fact that in Jesus Christ our humanity is no longer exiled or separated from God. Israel came home to Jerusalem, they would say, and we in our turn say that we have come home to God. The birth of this child has done away with the impassable gulf between humanity and God, just as Israel was able to do away with the endless miles between Babylon, where they were in exile, and Jerusalem, where they wanted to be. Isaiah gives us another way of expressing what this birth means. It tells us that we have come home, home to God, home to our true nature as creations of God. Perhaps it isn't an accident that all of us place such a tremendous emphasis on being home for this season if at all possible. Why not? The great news at the heart of Christmas is that we have come home in the deepest sense.

Gilbert Keith Chesterton expressed this in lovely lines.

> To an ancient house in the evening
> Home shall men come,
> To an older house than Eden
> And a taller town than Rome.
> To the end of the way of the wandering star,
> To the things that cannot be and that are,
> To the place where God was homeless
> And all men are at home.

We have had a feast of images. None of them on their own will fully express what Christians believe to be the meaning of this birth. In the end, very wisely, we always take refuge in simpli-

city. Listen to the words of carols. Almost always they have a
folk quality, an innocence, a simplicity. If we attribute that to a
past and simpler world, we would be wrong. Modern carols turn
for their inspiration to the same simplicity. Sometimes (and I think
here we are wisest) we turn to the quality of childhood, either
watching a children's pageant or standing before a crèche scene.
It is so simple that a child immediately knows what is there. It
is so profound that, as you turn from it as an adult, you are fully
satisfied.

What is being communicated by Christmas? The feast has so
many layers of meaning now that we have to remind ourselves
of the specific reality hidden in it. To say that it isn't just about
going home or gift giving or being kind or wishing people well,
is not in the least to dismiss these things. Even to say that it
celebrates the truth and loveliness and hope hidden in childhood
(while this is true) is not enough.

The heart of Christmas is certainly the child in the manger. It
is perfectly possible to take a deep religious meaning from the
season merely at this level. But one must never forget to ask the
question which lifts one's understanding of Christmas to the level
of Christian faith. The necessary question is deceptively simple.
We ask, "What child is this?" and faith answers, "This child is
God incarnate, God in human flesh."

Once we begin to use language like this, we are moving into
different territory. This is not just pleasantness or sentiment, but
an awesome fact being stated, an awesome claim being made.
The irony is, of course, that all those beloved carols make this
claim. They certainly take for granted the identity of the child as
divine. Somehow the immensity of what they are saying has been
filtered out, perhaps by familiarity.

Why is this claim for the identity of the child so important? First,
because Christians have claimed this from the very beginning.
Secondly, because the single great contribution of the Christian
faith to the world is to bring the news that the divine has come
into the human, that God is present in human history. Why is
this important? Because, if men and women are to retain the
capacity to live creatively within history, in spite of its terrors,
they need the reassurance that comes from the knowledge that
God shares that history. To believe that God has entered human
history in Mary's child is to know that God is not an infinitely

remote being who gazes from beyond time and space on a struggling self-threatened species called humanity.

To believe in the awesome fact of incarnation is to believe that the author of the human play has stepped into the play and is actor in it with us. The fact that, when he came on to the human stage, he did not choose a grandiose posturing heroic part, but instead played his lines as servant and peacemaker and finally as prisoner, makes his coming among us all the more wondrous and hopeful. This is precisely why the Christians began early to sum up their faith in an ancient Jewish word. They would say of Jesus that he is *Emmanuel*, which means "God with us."

Christmas

An Opening of Gifts

I will greatly rejoice in the Lord, my soul shall exult in my God; for he has clothed me with the garments of salvation, he has covered me with the robe of righteousness, as a bridegroom decks himself with a garland, and as a bride adorns herself with her jewels. Isaiah 61:10

But when the time had fully come, God sent forth his Son, born of woman, born under the law. Galatians 4:4

In the beginning was the Word, and the Word was with God, and the Word was God. He was in the beginning with God; all things were made through him, and without him was not anything made that was made. In him was life, and the life was the light of men. The light shines in the darkness, and the darkness has not overcome it.

There was a man sent from God, whose name was John. He came for testimony, to bear witness to the light, that all might believe through him. He was not the light, but came to bear witness to the light.

The true light that enlightens every man was coming into the world. John 1:1–9

He took him up in his arms and blessed God and said, ''Lord, now lettest thou thy servant depart in peace, according to thy word; for mine eyes have seen thy salvation.'' Luke 2:28–30.

I want you to ask yourself a question that sounds simple. It isn't really. But then most of the great questions in the Bible sound simple when, of course, they are profound. Here is the question. What happened a few days ago on that day we call Christmas?

For almost everybody, particular things happened, even if for some they happened only on the surface of life. There was a meal, perhaps a midnight act of worship, an exchanging of gifts, a singing of carols, a sense of joyful and precious interlude in the busyness and strain of life. There may have been a saying of certain words, words like "unto us a child is born; unto us a child is given" or "those who walk in darkness have seen a great light."

In what sense did any more than that happen? Perhaps another way of putting the question would be to ask at what depth those things happened if they did happen. Was there at all a sense of something or someone coming to birth inside us? Was there at all an awareness of something new happening, a sense of new directions we might take? Was there any sense of light coming on inside us, a light that might allow us to take more steps, to continue searching, to live with a little more joy and a little more meaning in a world that isn't the simplest of worlds and in a time that isn't the easiest of times. I ask these things because that is precisely why this season is given to us. It is why we are given the memory of this birth in the wintertime of the year in our northern world. We are given it so that it may trigger birth in us and be a light to us.

Let's look at the passages of scripture we've just read. They are exciting, and they can be immensely creative for us. We have just listened to Isaiah, one of the world's greatest poet-prophets. He bids people "rejoice and exult." Why? Because God has done three things. God has "clothed us with the garments of salvation," and God has "covered us with the robe of righteousness." Again, God will cause "righteousness and praise to spring forth before all nations." What meaning does that language have for us? It seems to me that, if God has clothed me with salvation, then in this Christmas season God had given me something that saves me from failure in my daily struggle to be human and to be Christian. God, in this child of Christmas, has been born again in me! I am saved from a sense of failure, and I am given new meaning and joy in my life.

When I read that God has "covered me with a robe of righteousness," I realize that I am less naked in the experiences of my daily life. That does not mean that I claim some invulnerability to life, that I think of myself as different from, or superior to, other people. Saying that I am less naked because God has done something for me is merely claiming that I possess a grace that can be a resource to me as I grapple with life. To put it in very simple words: as I look at the holy child shown to me, I realize that I too am a child of God. I am many other things. I may be very much adult. I may be parent, professional, employer, employee, spouse. But the thing which wraps all these up, the thing which can help me to get all the others right, is the realization that, above all else, I am a child of God.

We hear, too, in these scriptures that "God shall make righteousness and praise spring forth before all the nations." Does that seem a present actuality? Does the content of the television news, the daily paper, the radio seem to portray righteousness and praise springing forth before the world? Of course not. Then is the phrase in scripture merely long-ago unreal religious language? Or is it possible that God, in this season and with this birth of our Lord Jesus Christ, has lifted the veil that separates us from that kind of world and given us entry to it for this one glorious day? The importance of seeing it like this is that such a day can give us the courage and hope to go on working and sacrificing for the kind of world described by Isaiah, a world where righteousness and praise do spring forth before all nations.

Let's turn now to what Saint John said to us today. You and I can be so familiar with these words that we can miss the good news in them. John lists three magnificent things that can be true of you and of me. He says that you and I are alive with God's life, that we are bearer's of God's light, and that you and I can, if we choose, embody God to the extent that a human life can — always realizing that only our Lord could do so ultimately. You and I are alive with God's life. Savour that fact. Feel the way it can change our self-image. We are ordinary, of the stuff we call humanity. But we are more, so much more. Each of us is a place where God has deigned to dwell.

Carl Jung says that you and I have what he called a shadow. There is a dark side to our being and to our living. We know that all too well. Scripture is very realistic about it. Christian faith does not deny it for one moment. But scripture and Christian faith say that you and I are also bearers of God's light, carriers of a divine flame that can never be extinguished. "The light," says Saint John, "shines on in the darkness, and the darkness has not overcome it."

We Christians say that the word *gospel* means good news. Isn't it good news to be told in sacred scripture that there is in you a flame of God that nothing can put out? We all know that life asks us to face fierce and terrible winds that blow in our deepest experiences. Things happen that threaten to tear us apart. But we are assured that, at the centre of our deepest being, there is a flame of the living creating God that is there for ever. The winter of pain or loss can numb our souls. It may threaten to cover us with the ice of agony or sorrow, but the flame lives, and therefore you and I live. Our capacity to act returns. We become again people who can love and be loved. The future lives in us, and tomorrow is possible.

It isn't only Saint John who speaks to us of light in this season. Saint Luke in the gospel speaks of the day when Mary and Joseph took the child to the temple to present him before the Lord. Out from the shadows comes the old man Simeon. He lifts the child high in his arms and sings out his joy; he has seen the light he has been waiting for all his life.

In this season God brings you and me from the shadows of our ordinary living, presents us with the Christ child, and waits for our eyes and hearts and voices to register the fact that we realize we have seen again the coming of a light to our fearful and frantic age. As we watch old Simeon singing his joy, as we celebrate in our own way the joy of this season, God asks us to hold his Son in our arms, to carry him into our living, to embrace the gift of this glory.

Look now at the piece of Saint Paul's letter which we read. Paul is trying to communicate something very important about human experience. We grow. We must grow or we are in trouble. To be a human being is to experience physical, mental, and spiritual development. That is true of other aspects of our lives. It is true of the development of our professional skills. But we can easily forget that it must also be true of our lives in God. We cannot remain static. We must grow, develop, mature. If we are not growing in our relationship with God in Christ, then we are actually diminishing.

Paul sets out to emphasize one aspect of our relationship with God. He says that religion begins with rules and ''shoulds'' and ''musts.'' It begins as law, but it must develop at some stage into a relationship. We may begin by obeying the will of God because we feel we have to, but we grow towards obeying God because we want to. In Paul's image, we move from being slaves on the estates of God to becoming the sons and daughters of the owner!

How does this happen? It happens through Jesus Christ. He has given us our relationship with God by taking on our humanity, by accepting its sinfulness, by redeeming it through his life, death, and resurrection, and then by presenting it to God.

We have been thinking about such things as realizing who we really are, about growing and maturing in our faith. The world is full of stories that tell of such self-discovery. It's easy to miss the profound and eternal truth in those stories because we associate them with childhood. Cinderella discovers she is really a princess. The slave in the castle discovers he is the king's son. Notice that it almost always happens when somebody begins to love them. Who is the person whose love releases us from being merely who we thought we were, to become the person we really are? Jesus Christ.

Let's go back to where we started. We asked ourselves a question. We wondered what happened, what really happened inside us on that day of days we call Christmas. We've turned to a number of people to tell us what might happen. Isaiah told us that at Christmas you and I were given new clothes. Their brand name, if you will, is "Salvation." So let's put them on and start living in them. The other thing that God has done is to present before the eyes of the whole world something utterly good and beautiful and true, the child who is his Son, whose birth we celebrate.

Saint John said that the light of God is actually shining in you and in me, that you and I are actually being energized by that inner light, and that nothing can extinguish it. It can be on the point of going out when it flares up again. Good news? That's magnificent news! That news can encourage us and transform our ability to work, to serve, to live.

Saint Luke in a sense asked us to dance our joy at the realization of what has happened again at this season. He showed us old Simeon dancing and singing, and thereby asked us to make our faith a thing of celebration, something powerful that becomes young again because of this holy birth.

Saint Paul asked us to look again at our religion and see it as a relationship with God through Christ. Yes, it has rules, but ultimately it is far more than rules. It has obligations, but ultimately it is not merely about obligations. It is about growing in relationship with a loving God who has come towards us in Jesus

Christ, his hand outstretched to draw us into relationship. Yes, there is obedience involved, obedience and responsibility and accountability — as there is in any relationship worth the name — but it can be an obedience that we accept, not because we have to but because we want to.

At this season, then, we are given a gift. As Isaiah says, we are given a child. We have thought together about the gifts which are ours because of that child. Take the gifts home. Open them. Enjoy them. Live them. Because to live them is to taste, here and now, the strange mysterious reality we call eternal life.

A Coming of Kings

Now when Jesus was born in Bethlehem of Judea in the days of Herod the king, behold, wise men from the East came to Jerusalem, saying, "Where is he who has been born king of the Jews? For we have seen his star in the East, and have come to worship him." When Herod the king heard this, he was troubled, and all Jerusalem with him; and assembling all the chief priests and scribes of the people, he inquired of them where the Christ was to be born. They told him, "In Bethlehem of Judea; for so it is written by the prophet. 'And you, O Bethlehem, in the land of Judah, are by no means least among the rulers of Judah; for from you shall come a ruler who will govern my people Israel.' "

Then Herod summoned the wise men secretly and ascertained from them what time the star appeared; and he sent them to Bethlehem, saying, "Go and search diligently for the child, and when you have found him bring me word, that I too may come and worship him." When they had heard the king they went their way, and lo, the star which they had seen in the East went before them, till it came to rest over the place where the child was. When they saw the star, they rejoiced exceedingly with great joy; and going into the house they saw the child with Mary his mother, and they fell down and worshiped him. Then, opening their treasures, they offered him gifts, gold and frankincense and myrrh.
Matthew 2:1–11

Near the end of the Second World War, William Temple, then archbishop of Canterbury, was conducting a mission to the University of Oxford. One morning in a Bible study he deliberately threw a sudden question to provoke thought. He asked, "Do you think God knows anything about atomic fission?" There was silence. Afterwards, talking about the reaction and the response, the group admitted that almost everyone's first reaction was, "How could he, because it happened since his time!"

It is so easy for us all, with utmost loyalty and good intentions, to think of the things of faith as being essentially past things. Great things, magnificent things, but past.

Let's be quite clear about the Bible. It comes to us from history. It introduces us to faces and voices of history. But the Bible as sacred writing is not merely about the past. Neither, by the way, is it a kind of magic talisman for telling the future. It is, however, an incomparable insight into the human situation, an insight so profound that it is of universal and eternal application. It introduces men and women to themselves in every generation. Its faces are our faces. Its voices are our voices.

To illustrate this let me tell you a single Bible story, but in three ways. It is the central image and event in the Christian imagination at this time of year. First, we hear it as a man told it twenty centuries ago.

Now when Jesus was born in Bethlehem of Judea in the days of Herod the king, behold, wise men from the East came to Jerusalem saying, "Where is he who has been born king of the Jews? For we have seen his star in the East, and have come to worship him."

Then Herod summoned the wise men secretly and ascertained from them what time the star appeared; and he sent them to Bethlehem, saying, "Go and search diligently for the child, and when you have found him bring me word."

When they saw the star, they rejoiced exceedingly with great joy; and going into the house they saw the child with Mary his mother, and they fell down and worshipped him. Then, opening their treasures, they offered him gifts, gold and frankincense and myrrh.

Such is the ancient and lovely telling. Now, let's look at some facts which may lie behind that. One night in the seventeenth century Johannes Kepler, the astronomer, looked through his telescope and saw in the skies of Europe a bright light. He knew it to be something which occurs every 800 years. Kepler knew that the same light had occurred in the night sky when an ancient, distant king called Herod was desperately guarding his waning power. It was the coming together of Jupiter and Saturn in the constellation of the Fish. Kepler said to a friend that the light could have been the star of the magi. People were either shocked or amused. Not until recent times did we discover the ancient Star Almanac of Sipper. In it is listed, correct to the day, the star movements of the year we call 7 B.C. That year a Persian astronomer looked into the clear skies and saw what Kepler would see seventeen centuries later. For that man, however, the stars spoke. In his world Jupiter was the star of a world ruler, Saturn that of Palestine, the Fish constellation spoke of a last or crisis time. He knew what he had to do.

They headed west and south, coming down eventually from the high plateau where, twenty centuries later, Americans would die trying to rescue other Americans held hostage. They crossed the wide valley of the Euphrates, endured the desert miles beyond that, forded a small river called Jordan, climbed the rock wall of the escarpment, and saw the walled city below them. There they had a chilling encounter with a syphilitic paranoid butcher, the repulsive wreckage of a once great and charming statesman named Herod the Great. And one day, checking carefully if they were being followed, they came to a place of poverty and of great and sacred beauty, where they knelt before a peasant family and offered symbolic gifts.

That is to tell the story for the second time and in a second way. Now, let's take that story away from the pages of a book (the Bible) and from the plains of Persia. Let each one of us now, by an effort of the imagination, take the story with all its images and voices and events, and relocate it in the inner landscape of our own ongoing experience, deep in the mysterious country which is our personal interior life. Make yourself the stage on which the drama takes place. Now ask what it means in that interior personal country, very much as we might dream a dream and in the morning ask ourselves what it might mean for our waking lives. As we might try to recapture the main images of the dream, so let us capture the images of the story.

When Jesus was born in Bethlehem . . . Herod was king.

A child is being born at the same time as a death dealing power rules. But isn't that a capsule description of the world of the 1980s? A new world is desperately trying to be formed out of the disintegration of an old. At the same time that birth is over-shadowed by the possibilities of the power of nuclear death.

In such an age as ours, what is wisdom? What do wise men and women choose as an attitude? What do they look for? They look, in a world which many think is dying, for every possible sign of birth. In contemporary skies, which for many are darkened by psychological clouds of despair and physical clouds of technological holocaust, wise men and women look for the presence of even a single star, a single element of hope, possibility, breakthrough.

They said, "We have seen his star. . .and we have come."

People who are ready to adopt an attitude of hope, who look for the star in this late century, know that they will have to journey, to change, to search. Today, if we would seek wisdom, we cannot stay where or as we are. Every single one of us has had to journey through uncharted experience. Many of us have had to change psychologically and mentally to remain effective as professionals. Some of us have had to search desperately for resources within ourselves. In every society political theory is having to change radically in response to new realities. The church is having to search for new ways of ministry in a different world.

Wise men came to Jerusalem . . . Herod was troubled.

Inside us, what might the symbol of Jerusalem mean? Jerusalem is the city. The city can signify all the complexity and ambiguity of contemporary experience. It can mean all the anxiety, all the pressures, all the fragmentation which sometimes threaten to disintegrate us. Sometimes we can feel that these death-dealing elements in human experience are out to destroy us. In that sense their collective name is Herod! Herod signifies all that which, given a chance, would destroy human hope and commitment and motivation, and would bring our journey as persons or as a society to an end. Wise men and women know that you cannot avoid "Jerusalem," and "Herod" is always to be encountered.

"Tell me," said Herod, "when you have found the child. . . ."

Herod tries to co-opt the wise men to betray their journey, to end their commitment to the future possibility, to kill the child. Today, if you try to be a questing human being of hope, if you are committing yourself in some way to the quality of God's future — it may be in a political party, a voluntary organization, an institution — there are many ways in which Herod speaks. The "Herod" voice says, "Why invest your energy in idealistic dreams? Why be naïve? Acknowledge that survival is the name of the game. Why not make what you can from the wreckage?"

So speaks Herod in our weariness and discouragement, and in much of our time and society. If we are wise, we do what the wise men did. We hear the voice of the old king of death and fear and cynicism, but we go our own way. They went their way, and because they refused to be seduced by cynicism, the star they had committed themselves to appeared again. You see, if we commit ourselves to the God who calls us to journey, to the God who calls us to search for that which shines as the ultimate value in our experience, that ultimacy, that star, that light of God haunts us and draws us and calls us.

A final image, a coming home. The wise men came to where the child was, and they gave their gifts. If our journeying and searching have been in response to the God who calls us, we come at length to the place where we discover a child. Who and where is that child? That child is the new man or woman God is calling you and me to become.

It is for the birthing of that child inside yourself that God wishes you to give your gifts. Your gold, your frankincense, your myrrh are such things as your energy, your integrity, your brain, your loyalties, your hope, your deepest elements of heart and mind and soul and strength. For when you allow the child within you to be born, then you are re-energized to bring the child of hope and possibility and new creation to be born at every other level. This can be true in your relationships, in your profession, in your society, in your country, in the world of your time. Thus, through you, the eternal and holy child of hope and possibility, who is Christ Jesus our Lord, can be born daily, not in a remote past but in the present.

Do you see a great and mysterious thing? You are the story. You yourself are the child of God who is daily being called into birth. You yourself are also the wise man or woman seeking the child. You yourself are the living, breathing Bethlehem in which the Christ child is continually being born.

Epiphany

A Dream of One World

"Behold, the former things have come to pass, and new things I now declare; before they spring forth I tell you of them." Isaiah 42:9

And Peter opened his mouth and said: "Truly I perceive that God shows no partiality, but in every nation any one who fears him and does what is right is acceptable to him." Acts 10:34–35

When the child was born to Mary, a strange thing happened. Visitors, unknown, exotic, unexpected, came and knelt with gifts. Their coming seemed to be a hint, even a warning. It seemed to warn that, while this birth seemed merely a rustic, local event, it was more. While it seemed to be within Judaism, it was somehow also beyond it. The stable and the village were greater than they seemed, they were capable of being inclusive of much more.

I emphasize that word *inclusive*. It is the theme of this reflection. It would become an immense and painful issue in those first years of the movement that came to be called Christian. Among other things, it would entirely change the lives of a Roman and a Jew. In the tenth chapter of the book of Acts we meet them.

At the moment you and I enter this story, it is about two years since a terrible crucifixion and an electrifying resurrection near Jerusalem. A community has developed. Its leaders are those who know Jesus of Nazareth best. These leaders are moving across the country as they get requests from a group here, a community there, a family, an individual.

Peter has left Jerusalem and is staying with a friend in the seacoast town of Joppa. Today, just north of this spot, the Mediterranean reflects the high-rise apartment towers and hotels of Tel Aviv. As we travel some miles north of here, the high-rises fade into centuries of time. We are soon in open country. Eventually on our left is a golden, curving beach. Along the shoreline behind the beach is a length of well-preserved dark masonry, an old aquaduct. It is broken in places. Through its great arches you can see the Mediterranean. Walk out on the beach. Herod had one of his sons murdered on this beach. Push your foot into the gravel at low tide and you may pick up a piece of worn mosaic from a long-gone Roman villa.

Now eliminate 1900 years. You are on a quay side. The aquaduct is still behind you, but now it is shining and new, patrolled by Roman security police. The curving arms of a magnificent breakwater circle an artificial harbour. Out at the end is a tower, at night a lighthouse. Head back into the streets. We are searching for a certain house, a modest house. Non-commissioned officers don't get high pay although they are the back bone of the army. We are at the home of Gaius Cornelius, centurion in the tenth legion. He is a thoughtful and sensitive man. He wants a future for his family, and he wants to give them something worthwhile to believe in. For his generation, faith in anything beyond the empire itself and its army is fragile.

Very often Cornelius finds himself in the local synagogue. For such as he there is a special seating area. The Jewish community had a word for such visitors. They called them "Godfearers," searchers for meaning, God-hungry Greeks and Romans who were attracted to Judaism and sometimes actually joined. Cornelius gives generously to this synagogue. He is attempting to have a prayer life. At the deepest levels of his being he is very hungry.

Even by the sea Caesarea can be hot in high summer. For many mid-afternoon is siesta time. In that sleep Cornelius dreams. It is a dream of light, of encounter, and of illumination. He wakes knowing that he simply must act. He has heard of a particular Galilean rabbi. He knows the army has had to crucify him, but then it was one crucifixion among many. Continuing rumours and the occasional conversation have raised his curiosity. He has been wanting to find out more. Now he must. Within hours three of his men are riding south to Joppa with an invitation to Peter to come to Caesarea as guest.

Twenty-four hours after the three leave, while they are still approaching Joppa, Peter is on his friend's shaded roof-top area.

He is praying quietly. He nods asleep, and because his body is thinking of lunch (it's about the third hour, noontime) he has a vivid and disturbing dream. He is looking at a gargantuan container, resembling a net. In it is every conceivable kind of living creature. A voice says, "Peter, kill and eat." The hunter in him is called. But the Jew in him holds back. What is clean? What is unclean? What is allowed? Not allowed? Then comes the piercing insight. They are all God's creation. Why regard some as unclean? Why not accept all? Three times the net is lowered. Peter wakes to the sound of people downstairs. Dazed and confused he hears the invitation to Caesarea. He hears his own voice accepting, not quite understanding why.

A day later Peter finds himself being welcomed by an eager, excited group. As a Jew he has never been among Romans in this easy social way. Suddenly, he connects his dream and this encounter. His view of the world shatters. There can be no more clean and unclean, acceptable and unacceptable, outsiders and insiders, Jew and Gentile. Peter feels a new wholeness, a new inclusiveness sweep over him. In a moment he is speaking about his Lord and friend. He can see Cornelius and the others drinking in what he is saying. The day ends with baptism, tears, laughter, hospitality. The Holy Spirit has come to this house, a Gentile house, an enemy house. For Peter, and for some others in that tiny early Christian world, it is the first glimpse of a larger and suddenly limitless world. The shell has broken. The new faith has grown wings.

Long ago? Yes. Why tell it? Because it is about us. In what way? Consider. Human history could be written around the theme of moments when our human vision of the way God acts in history has suddenly had to broaden and grow. We are at such a moment. At countless levels we wrestle with the painful demands on our capacity to include rather than exclude. Look at the many levels of that demand. First, very near home. In this century Christians of different traditions have created some links across denominations. That is a tiny step on the journey from Joppa to Caesarea. Secondly, over the last century, in agonized slowness yet with deliberation, race has reached out to race. That mutual inclusion and acceptance, God knows, is far from complete. But at least we are on the road. Thirdly, in the last decade we are realizing that there must be a new reaching out across the three great visions which came from the desert, each of which has the allegiance of untold millions — Judaism, Islam, Christianity. We do not know how. All we know is that we must, if tragedy is to be put behind us and if there is to be a future of peace.

Beyond the merely religious, in the institutional sense, let me mention three mysterious and intriguing hints we are being given that something or someone awe-inspiring is calling us to include rather than exclude.

It is most certainly true that within a single generation a new inclusiveness is being called into being within the many-faceted mystery and spectrum of our human sexuality. Again, ecologically, a mysterious process is drawing us into an increasingly intimate relationship with certain creatures, particularly the great whales and the dolphin. Even beyond that we may consider the exponentially growing network of communications being woven over the planet like a web. Some minds think it possible that there is gradually coming into being a total human consciousness far beyond present imagination. That possibility was part of the vision of that gentle genius, priest, and scientist, Pierre Teilhard de Chardin. He spoke of the forming of a single and infinitely rich human consciousness indwelt by the Holy Spirit of God. It is a mystery he called the hominization of the world.

We have come a long way from the home of Cornelius where he and Peter meet, where God calls them to stretch out towards one another across a great gulf of race, religion, and culture. Yet, let me suggest how the Holy Spirit of God reveals such mysteries to our twentieth century. We have seen how Peter went up on a roof top. Ancient Joppa stretched along the shore. The jagged hills of Judea rose behind him against the sky. There on that roof top Peter slept and dreamed of a new inclusive vision of creation. In our lifetime there was a man who, by a staircase of technological fire, went beyond the roof of the world. Travelling in a rhythm of sleeping and waking, he stood eventually on the silent desert of the moon. There he pointed a camera at the jagged lunar horizon. Thus he saw a vision very like that which Peter saw.

Do you recall Peter's vision? A great net seemed to come from the sky. It contained all kinds of living things. The voice which spoke to Peter demanded his respect for this creation which was being offered to him. In the vision which the eye of that camera gave us all, a vast and lovely net appeared over that barren horizon of the moon. The earth rose breathtakingly lovely, mighty yet fragile, poised against the black backdrop of space. For the first time we saw the terrestrial net which carries all life as we know it.

That vision has changed and is changing us as Peter's vision and Cornelius's vision changed them. That vision is changing our view of humanity. It is affecting our relationship with the created order around us. Such change must surely be the slow majestic prompting of the same Holy Spirit of God which brought Peter to the home of Cornelius long ago. As the epiphanies of this decade come to us, we ask a question. To what house of unimagined unity and inclusiveness is the Holy Spirit leading us?

Epiphany

A Future People

To me, though I am the very least of all the saints, this grace was given, to preach to the Gentiles the unsearchable riches of Christ, and to make all men see what is the plan of the mystery hidden for ages in God who created all things; that through the church the manifold wisdom of God might now be made known to the principalities and powers in the heavenly places. This was according to the eternal purpose which he has realized in Christ Jesus our Lord, in whom we have boldness and confidence of access through our faith in him. So I ask you not to lose heart over what I am suffering for you, which is your glory. Ephesians 3:8–13

Part of the genius of the Bible is its brutal honesty. It records patterns of spirituality with the same dispassion as medical technology scans the human body. As technology delineates both diseased and healthy tissue with the same precision, so the Bible reveals sick spirituality and saintliness or grace with the same clarity. Just as medical technology exposes physical weakness so that resources may be gathered for bodily repair, so the sometimes terrible analysis of scripture reveals spiritual vulnerability so that a way may be opened for grace and healing.

Consider how consistently in the Bible men and women whom we first meet as seeming spiritual giants must at some stage be stripped of their strengths — must stand naked and vulnerable, confessing their inability to carry out an assigned task — only to find an undreamed of grace to return to their responsibilities. Moses, the would-be great leader, bellows his impotence and frustration to the sun-scorched rocks of a wilderness which is both around and inside him. Elijah, the would-be prophetic champion of God, wallows in self pity, depression, and paranoia in his cave, a cave both psychological and geographical, on the slopes of Horeb. Paul, the would-be heresy hunter and guardian of orthodoxy, scrambles desperately to get away from the flailing legs of a terrified horse as he grovels in blind concussion, this man who saw so much so clearly, on the Damascus road.

Yet every one of them, far from being destroyed by the recognition of their own dependency, finds that the experience of a deep sense of powerlessness creates for them an energy and motivation. It enables them to re-enter the very arena from which they have recoiled in rage or depression or terror.

Consider Paul as he writes to the community in Ephesus. (He writes also beyond Ephesus, because we are fairly certain this is a letter for general circulation.) Paul speaks as a prisoner. But, of course, so do we all. We are prisoners of our own humanity: our fears, our lack of self-worth, our resentments. We are no less prisoners of the cultural assumptions of our society even though we are politically free. We are, with every single member of the human family, most certainly prisoners of the technology of annihilation which we have ourselves assembled, and on whose fiery altar we and other great empires are sacrificing the resources which should be available for compassion and social justice.

On a personal level Paul roamed the empire, yet he carried everywhere the claustrophobic cell of chronic illness and guilt about the past. Yet, precisely because he is able to let a deep sense of inadequacy surface and be expressed — ''I am the least of all the saints'' — he is given the grace to look at the pitiable little groups and communities created so raggedly and haphazardly across a vast urban empire and, in full awareness of the complex and sophisticated structures of empire, to claim something entirely laughable. Of those pathetic faith communities he says, ''Through the church the manifold wisdom of God might now be made known to the principalities and powers.'' Any intelligent Roman politician hearing that could be excused for curtly diagnosing a case of simple delusion.

Yet Paul, by a grace given to him, was able to see a potential energy in those small groups of Christians, tiny minorities in the cities of the empire. There were many reasons for his ability to see this. Perhaps the most powerful reason was that in Jesus Christ he had himself seen that which was considered weak become stronger than the strongest. He had seen one who was thought dead standing in power and risen life before him. That had changed Paul's life. It had transformed the old Saul into the new Paul. He realized how that new life had remained hidden within himself after the death of Stephen, bursting out with blinding intensity on the Damascus Road.

He knew, too, how he had buried himself in the lonely room in Damascus, his neat, arrogant world shattered, his whole being realizing for the first time what it meant not to be in charge, not to be independent. He remembered how the touch of Ananias's hand and the sound of Ananias's timid voice calling "brother" had called him to life again. Even after that, Paul could recall the years he had had to bury himself in the desert, remaining hidden to all but a few who could trust in his new allegiance to Jesus Christ. From that temporary death he had again been called back to life by such friends as Peter.

So Paul was a man who knew much about having to die, having to remain hidden, having to wait for power and guidance. He had experienced it all. Because of this experience Paul was a man who knew the way God works. First there is a seed. That must go into the ground. It must remain hidden, sometimes ignored and forgotten. But in the turning of the earth and the sun there comes a time when the green shoot bursts into view and begins to grow high and tall. So Paul could look at the tiny Christian groups and see them as seeds buried in the furrow-like streets of Roman and Greek and Jewish cities. By some ignored, to some invisible and irrelevant, to Paul they are the seeds of the future, buried, like the Lord's body, only for a while before a new day. Paul knew that their time in obscurity and shadow would become a time of breaking into the life of the empire, into the light of day.

Paul saw even more. Somehow, even while the early Christian movement seemed a tiny weak minority, he was able to anticipate its ability to engage the immense powers of the empire. For Paul the future held the prospect of a prophecy he could recall from his people's early scriptures. As a small boy he would have heard the words of Isaiah being read in the synagogue, telling of the coming of kings in search of the rising of a new light, a new focus for all humanity, a new people in history. Paul found himself linking with that ancient vision a story that fellow Christians had handed on to him when he had first met them as a friend and as a new follower of their Lord. They had told him how visitors had come from far-away rich, sophisticated Persia.

They had brought gifts. They had inquired about a new birth, a new regime. In their journey, in their gifts, in their questions the prophecy of Isaiah had become uncannily true.

"Arise," Isaiah had sung to a people hidden, buried in exile, "Arise, shine; for your light has come . . . nations shall come . . . and kings." Paul sang the same song to the early Christian groups. Their task, like that of Isaiah's kings or Matthew's magi, was the bringing of gifts. The Christians were to become bearers of gifts to the world of their time. What would those gifts be? "The unsearchable riches of Christ." Who would one day have to confront these spiritual riches? The "principalities and powers."

We have been with Paul in that long-ago prison cell as he wrote to the Christian community in Ephesus. We have for a moment seen ourselves in the prison of our contemporary world. As we link those two prisons, we have to ask if we can envision, as Paul did, an empowerment of Christian faith in our time. As we struggle with that question, we might remember that Paul was under no illusion that the future would be won without cost.

As a Jew he would have been very much aware of the cost that must be paid to make the lyrical hope of Isaiah come true. For Isaiah the hope was a liberated, shining Jerusalem, a people in freedom, free in their own city again. But to achieve that meant sacrifice, long journeying, surveying against enemies, building among ruins. It meant bringing life out of death. As a follower of the risen Christ, Paul knew what the cost of the magi's visit had been. For them, long journeying, danger, the confrontation with the unpredictable Herod. For others, innocent and uninvolved, the sword at their children's throats.

Paul knew that future visions always have a cost. The terrible payment of the cross had bought the shattering victory of resurrection. He himself had paid many times in his life lived for Christ. These groups of Christians in Ephesus and Corinth and Jerusalem, in Alexandria and Lystra, and even in Rome itself would all pay a price. But the price would purchase the future.

We, wherever we are, are a group of Christians. Paul would recognize us. He might be very hard on us because he demanded high standards. But he would not dismiss us with contempt. He would see us as seeds in the culture of our time. He might see us imprisoned in our own human failings, hidden and lost in a vast secularized culture. But he would certainly see us as the seeds of a possible future for Christ and the things of Christ. Without a moment's hesitation he would say to us what he said to the Christians in long-ago Ephesus. ''Through the church the manifold wisdom of God [must] be known. Have boldness and confidence of access through your faith in him.''

A last moment with Paul as he writes to Ephesus. When we hear Paul defining himself, because of real and past guilt and present weariness, as ''the least of all the saints,'' we are hearing our own inner voice. It tells us in our moments of weakness that qualitatively we are the least of all Christian generations. We do not, we feel, have the fire of the early church, the theological power of the Fathers, the mystic insight of the Middle Ages, the evangelical fervour of a previous century. Yet, notice how, in spite of his self-dismissal, Paul is enabled by grace to ''preach to the Gentiles . . . to make all see the plan of God.'' By exactly that same grace we, in the name of Christ and by the grace of Christ, can communicate with our present society.

Arise! shine! For in Jesus Christ your light has come.

Ash Wednesday

A Season of Shadows

"Thus, when you give alms, sound no trumpet before you, as the hypocrites do in the synagogues and in the streets, that they may be praised by men. Truly, I say to you, they have received their reward. But when you give alms, do not let your left hand know what your right hand is doing, so that your alms may be in secret; and your Father who sees in secret will reward you.

"And when you pray, you must not be like the hypocrites; for they love to stand and pray in the synagogues and at the street corners, that they may be seen by men. Truly, I say to you, they have received their reward. But when you pray, go into your room and shut the door and pray to your Father who is in secret; and your Father who sees in secret will reward you.

"And when you fast, do not look dismal, like the hypocrites, for they disfigure their faces that their fasting may be seen by men. Truly, I say to you, they have received their reward. But when you fast, anoint your head and wash your face, that your fasting may not be seen by men but by your Father who is in secret; and your Father who sees in secret will reward you. Matthew 6:2–6, 16–18

Blow the trumpet in Zion; sound the alarm on my holy mountain! Let all the inhabitants of the land tremble, for the day of the Lord is coming, it is near, a day of darkness and gloom, a day of clouds and thick darkness! Like blackness there is spread upon the mountains a great and powerful people; their like has never been from of old, nor will be again after them through the years of all generations. Joel 2:1–2

Working together with him, then, we entreat you not to accept the grace of God in vain. For he says, "At the acceptable time I have listened to you; and helped you on the day of salvation." Behold, now is the acceptable time; behold, now is the day of salvation. We put no obstacle in any one's way, so that no fault may be found with our ministry, but as servants of God we commend ourselves in every way. 2 Corinthians 6:1–4

All over the world on a particular day, millions of men and women and children do an extraordinary thing. They enter a place of worship, kneel down at a brass or wooden or marble rail, look upward with their eyes closed, and they wait. They wait for another human being to come in front of each one of them carrying a small bowl full of black ashes. Those ashes have been made by burning some dried palm branches which a year ago were carried around in procession in the same place of worship.

The person carrying the bowl of ashes goes to each kneeling person, dips a thumb in the ashes, places the thumb on each forehead, and makes a rough sign of the cross on the skin. As this is done the person kneeling hears a devastating yet very simple statement: "You are dust and to dust you shall return."

Why do that extraordinary thing in our modern age? Some think it depressing, some think it primitive, even unhealthy! After all, we know we return to dust; do we really need literally to rub it in? We are terrified we will turn the whole planet to dust any day; do we need to drive that home so starkly? Yes, we do, for only by acting out something which one remembers from the dawn of the world, do we realize the tremendously important message we receive about ourselves and our destiny. In the second chapter of Genesis we read, "The Lord God formed man of dust from the ground." There, in that single statement, is the source of that strange piece of ritual which millions do on a day called Ash Wednesday.

But we need to go one sentence farther in that portion of Genesis to find out another reason, perhaps the real reason why we do this. After the dust was formed into human kind, we read that "God breathed into his nostrils the breath of life." No sooner does the Bible say that our humanity is dust than it tells us that God has breathed into our dust his divine life-giving breath. So something of immense importance has happened to that dust. It remains dust. Nothing changes that. But, because of God's breathing into it, that same dust is now made rich beyond measure with the divine life.

It is absolutely essential to realize that these two truths, sounded as part of the very opening act of the drama of creation, stand eternally together. They are inseparable. Because of their resilience in time and among human events, they have become the foundation of human hope for our human story. Because a human being is more than the physical entity we can see and touch and weigh and measure, then the person of a human being is given immense significance. A person is not mere object. A person is sacred. Yes, we hunt and maim and kill one another, and consequently as a race we are aware of incalculable guilt, because we know there is meaning to humanity beyond the physical.

Again, the fact of God breathing upon the dust which forms us gives us a deep source of hope for human nature. When we are faced with the dark side of our humanity, its sometimes revolting cruelties, we find it possible not to give up on human nature precisely because we are committed to the hope that the divine life dwells within it, even though in a particular situation the evidence against that possibility is chillingly obvious.

But, even if the Bible tells us that we are dust, why set out to remind ourselves year by year in a vivid act of liturgy? The answer is that we very badly need to be reminded. Even more so do we need this as the twentieth century goes on. Why? Because it is very deep in human nature, and particularly in our Western culture, to deny that we are dust. We don't, of course, use that language, but we say the same thing in different ways. We have a thousand ways to reassure ourselves that we are in charge of our own destiny, that we are more and more in charge of our own humanity. We find it easy to slip into seeing ourselves as being in charge of nature itself.

But paradoxically there is a sense in which such things are true. To be responsible for the created order is the vocation given to us by God. To regard ourselves as responsible for our future, responsible for the very human race itself and the very planet itself, is not arrogance but recognition of the truth. But all such human responsibility depends on one immense condition, that we never forget that we too are creatures, children of the same Majesty who formed the planet and the suns and galaxies which surround us. In that sense, created and formed, given the gift of life, we are dust. Brilliant dust? Yes. Creative, thinking dust? Yes, but still dust. For all the brilliance and creativity and thought and imagination within that dust are the shimmering traces of that divine breath within us.

That simple action performed every Ash Wednesday, that thumb imprint of burnt ashes on our brows, the words in our ears, are a reminder that, if we become mesmerized by our magnificent achievements, our awe-inspiring discoveries, our accumulation of powers, we risk forgetting what we really are. If we do this, we reach for even greater powers, not as servants of the Creator but with the twisted urge to be ourselves creator. Once this happens, we are in terrible danger. Ash Wednesday, then, is a warning. As a generation we need that warning more than any generation ever alive before us. We need to realize we are dust, in the sense of being "creature," because we are the first generation since time began to have gained the ability to turn our planet to dust.

We do more than the simple liturgical action. We also read these passages of the Bible. The first voice we hear is that of a man who felt about his world something of the dread and anxiety we feel about ours.

Joel lived about four centuries before our Lord. He lived at a time when his people had fought their way back from exile, from invasion, and from the destruction of their beloved city. They had achieved much, and yet Joel felt that they had paid a high price in the process. They had gained quantitatively but they had lost qualitatively. Joel felt there would be a day of reckoning ahead, not merely on economic or military or political grounds, though all these factors might well be part of future events. Joel felt that God would demand a time of reckoning. He called that time "the day of the Lord." His description of the retribution is chilling. In the face of that he calls his society to reform itself, to realize its shortcomings, to turn home to its true self and to God.

That call of Joel is 2400 years old, yet it is as contemporary as today's headlines. No generation knows more than ours how dark and terrible the future can seem. As we wrestle with seemingly intractible moral demands, the consequences of ignoring those demands assume greater and greater menace, whether we are speaking of the cost to the natural order or the gulf between "have" and "have not" societies. We know only too well that it is not within the will of God that millions go hungry, that whole tracts of earth are writhing under the technology and chemicals of our human enterprise. We know that it is not within the will of God that humanity live under the shadow of its own ability to effect global extermination. All of these things and their potential consequences form a "day of the Lord" for us. All of these things are sufficient for us to sanctify a fast, call a solemn assembly, gather the people.

For us to "sanctify a fast" might well be to look to our own consumption, our personal diet, our national policies in food exportation. To "call a solemn assembly" might be to make sure that there is always available a forum in which the people of the world can at least dialogue with one another. To "sanctify the congregation" might well be to make sure that congregations be made aware that the issues of our time are not merely political and economic but also the things of God, a sacred agenda, matters which are as much for our prayers as the things of personal faith.

Saying this kind of thing — that the issues of today are the agenda for Christians — is to do what Paul does as he writes to the people in Corinth. He asks three things of them. In doing so he also asks us. He asks us first to "be reconciled with God." That can have deep meaning personally. It can mean aligning our personal will with that of God, handing our will and our desires over for God's use, making ourselves God's instrument. It can also mean reconciling ourselves as a people with God's will. It can mean placing ourselves under the will of God for a more just society. Surely justice is at the heart of God's will. The Bible emphasizes it again and again.

Paul asks next for our "working together with God . . . accepting God's grace." As we face the very real coming of a "day of the Lord," we need to hear again from Paul something said frequently in scripture. Again and again God calls humanity to work with him. In the Bible it is usually individuals, but it can also be a call to a whole people. Sometimes the individuals or the people refuse. They are afraid. They haven't got the inner resources. They don't know how. The reasons for refusal are varied. But God again and again offers grace so that the refusal can become acceptance — a *no* becomes a *yes*. That is what Paul is saying to us as individuals and as a Christian people.

Paul finally emphasizes the need to decide. Putting God off is asking for failure. Putting off aligning ourselves with his will is tantamount to refusal. Tomorrow is not a valid "time zone" in our relationship with God. What counts is today. What matters is now. What do I do now for God and with God? What decision do I make now to align my will with God's? Is it to be merely my will, or is it to be mine and God's placed together, in so far as I can understand God's will for me?

For a few moments we move from being with Paul to being with our Lord. He is in some public place teaching, and he is reflecting about the pattern of our personal religious practice. He is probing the mixture of motivations which all of us have in our inner lives. Who are we really being religious for? For him there were those who made a public spectacle of piety in the society of their time. Today we face quite another pattern. Most people today wish so much to keep their faith and its practice private that they almost never betray their Christian allegiance in any public aspect of their lives. The result is that very often two people will work together for years without realizing that both are Christian and that they would have appreciated being able to share insights and attitudes of faith in their mutual tasks.

Our Lord mentions three things every Christian is called to do: to give alms, to pray, and to fast. We may use different language. We may speak of "supporting worthy causes." We might call fasting "dieting" or a simple life-style. But the question our Lord asks is just as valid now as then. He is asking us that we be quite clear what our motivation is in doing such things. We can give to causes to build our own ego, to be well thought of as benefactors. We can support something financially to gain power in its affairs. We can pray merely as a therapeutic device. If we include meditation as prayer, there are whole industries in our world selling meditation techniques as personal therapy! God, under any name, Christ or otherwise, is for them totally incidental and quite irrelevant!

We can diet for reasons of health. That is not in the least unchristian. We are called to be good stewards of our health. But we need not delude ourselves that such dieting is necessarily fasting. We can refrain from food for reasons that are essentially vanity and self-worship. To fast is to restrain appetite for a particular motivation. To fast is to offer oneself to God, to accept a discipline and a call which comes from beyond the self. To fast is a form of serving God. In fact, that is what our Lord demands in all our activities. He demands from us God's service rather than self-service.

Scripture has given us our true self-image. We are dust, but dust which contains the life of God. We are called to be workers together with God in the present moment, aligning our will with God and receiving God's grace. This offering of our deepest self to God reaches into the pattern of all we do. We do what we do, not merely for ourselves but for God.

A Change of Perception

I saw in the night visions, and behold, with the clouds of heaven there came one like a son of man, and he came to the Ancient of Days and was presented before him. And to him was given dominion and glory and kingdom, that all peoples, nations, and languages should serve him. Daniel 7:13–14

When Moses came down from Mount Sinai, with the two tables of the testimony in his hand as he came down from the mountains, Moses did not know that the skin of his face shone because he had been talking with God. And when Aaron and all the people of Israel saw Moses, behold, the skin of his face shone, and they were afraid to come near him. Exodus 34:29–30

For we did not follow cleverly devised myths when we made known to you the power and coming of our Lord Jesus Christ, but we were eyewitnesses of his majesty. For when he received honour and glory from God the Father and the voice was borne to him by the Majestic Glory, "This is my beloved Son, with whom I am well pleased," we heard this voice borne from heaven, for we were with him on the holy mountain. 2 Peter 1:16–18

Now Peter and those who were with him were heavy with sleep, and when they wakened they saw his glory and the two men who stood with him. And as the men were parting from him, Peter said to Jesus, "Master, it is well that we are here; let us make three booths, one for you and one for Moses and one for Elijah" — not knowing what he said. As he said this, a cloud came and overshadowed them; and they were afraid as they entered the cloud. And a voice came out of the cloud, saying, "This is my Son, my Chosen; listen to him!" And when the voice had spoken, Jesus was found alone. And they kept silence and told no one in those days anything of what they had seen. Luke 9:32–36

We are in one of the world's most hostile terrains. The ground here seems to be made of rock, the air is dry, the earth underfoot is hard and unyielding. Over everything the mountain looms. Sometimes it seems to possess a life of its own. Up through its vast body comes the hot breath of the planet. At times, unpredictable and awe-inspiring, it belches fire and billowing smoke. To a human in the valleys and ravines around its base, it seems to be almost godlike.

To explore Sinai, even today and with a group, takes courage and endurance. To climb upward alone among its shadowed clefts in a period of its volcanic activity must have taken immense courage. But that is the measure of the man who is the centre of this scene. Many hours ago he disappeared into the rising wilderness of rock. Here among this wandering people he looms large. Moving up the jagged, torn slopes he is diminished, becoming pathetically tiny and vulnerable. His going leaves a sense of insecurity. Although there are frequent arguments over his policies, there is no illusion among the people that Moses is anything less than vital to this terrible journey they have all undertaken.

There is something about this man that defies analysis. He commands immense authority, yet he obviously is not hungry for power. In fact, he obviously regards himself as under authority. For Moses the rule of God is paramount, the presence of God is a natural sense in him. In what will take place on this mountain, particularly in what he will mean to this people on his descent, his name will forever be linked with the law of God.

Here we leave Moses and travel to other places and stand on another mountain top. First, we move far away from the Sinai Peninsula. We are in the flat shimmering heat of the Euphrates Valley. We see a great capital city of the ancient world at a time when empires are rising and falling in a turmoil of history. Our eyes are those of a gifted man named Daniel. He is a visionary, seeing deeply into the realities of his time. He is able to communicate his experience in vivid searing images which have intrigued and puzzled generations for century after century.

Our moment with Daniel gives us two visions which have particularly haunted all who read them. Daniel sees a figure of vast and ageless majesty seated on a throne. Surrounding the throne is an innumerable host of worshippers. Before this throne all creation comes under judgement. The focus shifts. There comes from beyond the horizon a figure, human in appearance but somehow more than human. He stands before the throne in obvious special relationship to its occupant. To him is given an authority above all others, eternal and limitless.

Again we move away, leaving the world of Daniel, emerging from the convoluted, vivid world of his visions. We are now in a very real world with another figure. Elderly and imposing, he conveys a calm wisdom born of long and hard experience. We are in the presence of the apostle Peter.

Decades have passed since the events by his beloved lakeside. He has roamed far. He has seen the original small community become a widespread, thrilling, sometimes threatened, network of communities. He knows there is not much left of life for himself. Now he wishes once again to impress upon this still young Christian movement the rock-like reality on which the faith is based. As Peter speaks of "cleverly devised myths," we can hear the sarcastic phrases thrown at the new faith by sophisticates of the surrounding culture. Peter, of course, realizes his own value to the still young movement. His is no second-hand story. He, Peter, stood with the Lord, walked with him, rowed a boat with him, argued with him, in a word, was his friend. Peter does not have to trace the Christian tradition, he is the tradition! You can sense the understandable pride when he speaks of being "eye-witnesses of his majesty."

As Peter writes this passage, he is no longer sitting at the writing table or dictating. His body may well be there, but in imagination and memory he is far away. Peter has gone back, back down the years to the days beside the lake when he shared a fishing license with his brother Andrew. No longer is Peter the patriarchial figure whom men and women all around the Mediterranean respect, even venerate, whose voice they listen for when their new faith is threatened by persecution. Peter is young again, and once more he is in Galilee where the hills surround the lake and the narrow streets of Capernaum echo with the traffic and commerce that make this lakeshore a hub of activity. Above all, Peter is once more walking with the friend who came into his life no more than a couple of fleeting years before and changed it for ever. Peter wants to follow again through the events which sealed his allegiance and convinced him that he walked with a human friend who was dear beyond words but who, in some terrible and mysterious sense, was more. In what sense Jesus was more, Peter would never fully understand, as you and I will never fully understand. But what Peter was now remembering with utmost clarity from those early days made it possible for him to walk among a new generation of Christians as a spiritual giant.

They had been moving around the north end of the lake. For the disciples, new and inexperienced, far from confident of their own abilities, it had been both frightening and exciting when the Master sent them out to preach the wisdom of God and to heal. It also transpired that the Master had come to the notice of Herod the tetrarch. That could mean danger. The news had spread that a pathetic supply of food had multiplied to satisfy a listening crowd. Then, suddenly, the shadows began to fall. He turned to them one day and seemed anxious to know what people were saying of him. Peter always remembered the electric moment when Jesus' eyes ranged around them and asked quietly, ''Who do you say that I am.'' To his astonishment Peter heard his own voice reply, ''The Christ of God.'' At the time he hardly knew what he was saying or why. It welled up from within him and had to be let out.

He remembered the incident a little over a week later. Now and again the Master would invite the little group of three, himself and James and John. Those were treasured times of real intimacy. They were, however, not entirely easy or comfortable, because Peter was learning more and more that his encounter with Jesus on the lakeshore had involved him in an extraordinary relationship. That day, responding to the invitation, the four of them left. Peter, noting the direction they were going, guessed that they were headed for Tabor. It was only a few miles outside Nazareth. From its summit you could see all of southern Galilee. The hours they passed together in that still and lovely place would remain imprinted on his memory as long as life was in him. When he did try to recall all that was said, all that was felt, he found himself recapturing a kind of dream. A week before they had come away together, Jesus had spoken of things ahead that none of them wished even to consider. Now, here on the green, wooded mountain, the lake in the distance, it seemed as if he wished to have them grasp once and for all what he was about, why he had asked them to form the community of disciples.

Speaking rapidly and passionately he traced the purposes of God through the millenia of their history. He spoke of the magnificence of the law given by Moses, the moral majesty of the prophets embodied in Elijah. So vividly was the design of God's purposes revealed, that Peter remembered distinctly seeing Jesus in that great sacred tradition, flanked by the two giants of Judaism yet somehow giving their work new purpose, new context. As the hours went on, as all of them realized the unique quality of these precious hours alone with him, it seemed to them as if Jesus radiated an energy, a quality of being, a blinding intensity that communicated to them a mysterious truth far beyond his words.

Afterwards, when they spoke of that day, they realized that in their deepest being they were being told with thunderous clarity that they were in the presence of one who himself stood in the indescribable presence of the creator God. Each was rooted to the spot, feeling at the same moment both terror and ecstasy. Peter recalled himself pleading that they stay longer, that they be allowed to shelter, perhaps to capture this unutterable beauty and joy and unity granted them for a fleeting and tantalizing hour. But there came again before his eyes the green hills and the still lake, and they moved silently down the slopes, their thoughts in turmoil, their bodies keeping an instinctive distance from the companion among them.

As long as Peter lived, that experience lived within him. The light that radiated from Jesus on that mountain never dimmed in the ensuing years. Decades later and a thousand miles away Peter would turn to that day when he not only witnessed transfiguration but experienced it. Its reality would become his reference point as he rallied the scattered communities across the empire. And what of us, who are today's recipients of that long-ago letter? What for us is the opportunity to share the transfiguring light that both blinded and gave vision to Peter? As with any great mystery, one must choose the simplest of language if one hopes to respond at all.

First, I must be aware that the invitation to walk with my Lord Christ on the mountain can come at any time, usually unexpected and unplanned. My prayer must be that I hear the invitation when it is given and that I have the grace to respond. There will be a day when an ordinary moment of worship becomes extraordinary, when wine on my lips and bread in my mouth communicate the wonder of his body and blood in a moment of illumination and conviction that is undeniable. There will be encounters and inner experiences when the mists which shroud my poor humanity from my Lord's glory will for one shining moment be removed, as indeed, undeservedly and unsought, they have been. Then there will again be the longing which Peter knew, to stay on the mountain top, to cling to the companionship, to remain at the fire, to respond to the radiance. But, as Peter found, it is also a thing of infinite satisfaction to return from the mountain top and, remembering its glory, to serve in the world. For the Lord of the mountain top is also encountered in the actions of my days and of yours.

A Shout of Hosannas

Have this mind among yourselves, which is yours in Christ Jesus, who, though he was in the form of God, did not count equality with God a thing to be grasped, but emptied himself, taking the form of a servant, being born in the likeness of men. And being found in human form he humbled himself and became obedient unto death, even death on a cross. Philippians 2:5–8

And when they drew near to Jerusalem, to Bethpage and Bethany, at the Mount of Olives, he sent two of his disciples, and said to them, "Go into the village opposite you, and immediately as you enter it you will find a colt tied, on which no one has ever sat; untie it and bring it." Mark 11:1–2.

As they went out, they came upon a man of Cyrene, Simon by name; this man they compelled to carry his cross. And when they came to a place called Golgotha (which means the place of a skull), they offered him wine to drink, mingled with gall; but when he tasted it, he would not drink it. Matthew 27:32–34

I want to share an intuition with you. I suspect that, as we move towards the end of the century, there will continue a deepening and reforming of all the great spiritualities of the planet. Among the possible changes within Christian spirituality will be a more intense involvement in this week of liturgical and mystical times, this week we call Holy Week. I suspect that its observance will be more intentional, more disciplined, more sustained. Men and women will regard it more and more as what it really is — a pilgrimage, a sequential majestic journey into the most profound levels of divine and human nature, taking us into a place of stygian darkness before bringing us into halls of almost inexpressible resurrection light.

First, a reminder of something you may already know. In the modern meaning of the word *biography*, the gospels are not biographies of Jesus of Nazareth. Proof of this is the way that all the four gospel writers treat this week. Take Mark's gospel. One third of that short book is about this week. Think of that concentration — one week in a life of thirty years. This device, used by all four writers, says to us that this week in Christian time is countdown. The intervals are more precisely measured out. Quite frequently specific hours begin to be mentioned. Towards the end of the week the gospel clocks of death and resurrection tick away sixty minutes to the hour. Cock crow by cock crow, act by act, decision by decision, hammer blow by hammer blow.

For Christians the mind of Christ, the mind who is the Incarnation and the living Word of God, is a mystery beyond our human exploration. That love and that knowledge, though we saw it in action among us, is not for us to analyse or evaluate. It is there for our reverence, our thanksgiving, and our worship. But Christian faith also speaks to us of the full humanity of Jesus. Therefore, we need not hesitate to assume that he felt as we feel, heard as we hear, feared as we fear, suffered as we suffer. Step by step, therefore, we can walk with Jesus of Nazareth during the days of this week.

All last week you work your way south by the river road. Like any traveller you are glad to see the palm trees of Jericho shimmering ahead in the heat. Lying somewhere in the shade you down a citrus drink. You then begin the long climb up the army road, up through the narrow wadis in the hills, climbing the escarpment. Probably you try to make the last few miles west to the welcoming house at Bethany before Friday at sundown. You feel at home. You know you are going to need friends. You try to rest, but it isn't really rest because now you are totally committed and there is no going back.

Sunday you make the first move. You leave the house, walk around the road to the south shoulder of the mountain. You come up into the morning sun and the city faces you. It clings to the jagged hills like an animal at bay, waiting to spring. They bring you the little donkey, the first ragged cheer rings out. Step by scrambling step you move out and down onto the stage of the cosmic drama. That night you come back exhausted.

Each day you continue that rhythm. From Bethany to Jerusalem, from friendship to confrontation, from affirmation to challenge. From the sun and shadow of the public courts in the early morning to a bed of exhaustion at night.

On Monday you feel a cold rage flood through you at the cynicism and manipulation of the temple foreign exchange booths, amassing their inflated currencies in the name of religion. Unable to restrain yourself you lunge and push. You hear yourself shouting your contempt and anger. You decide to retreat while you still can. Somehow you know it isn't yet time.

Tuesday and Wednesday you are here again. There is constant confrontation now. You know there is less and less to lose from confrontation. You can feel the agony of friends who helplessly watch, wanting desperately to stop the process. You know very well the rising murmur going on behind nearby windows and official doors. You are aware that a net is closing. You have decided there is no other way.

Thursday, you book the room because you suspect that otherwise it will be too late. By the time everyone is seated, you realize that there may be even less time than you thought. You take refuge in symbolic acts. They are a kind of vivid, penetrating shorthand. It is so desperately important that these others at the table understand something. The meal is an ancient play. Everybody at this table has known the story since childhood. It's called the king's banquet. It's an image of a transformed universe. But there is one thing that you simply must communicate. The rules are different for tonight and tomorrow and forever. From now on the king does not only call the banquet and preside over it, from now on — and how can you possibly get them to understand this — the king is also himself the meal. Even as your humanity forms the thought, you shudder. You are the wine, to be spilled blood-red by spear and spike and thorn.

And there is one other thing before you go into the night. You must get them to understand that their concepts of power are wrong. They must realize that the only real power is servanthood. Nobody will ever understand that paradox easily. And, because there are no words rich enough, you look around, go to the door, take the water jar and the towel. One by one you wash their feet, the hardened brown skin, feeling the dust and sweat on your fingers.

Out into the night. First utter loneliness, then paralyzing fear. Suddenly the footsteps and torches and, strangely, a kind of resigned peace. Night becomes day, faces appear out of the shadows, voices rise and fall, spitting questions, abuse, suspicion, hatred. You are hustled through empty, sleeping streets. There is the blinding blaze of light in Herod's lecherous and decadant atrium. You are aware of the clink of iron on stone amid shouted orders in the corridors of Pilot's assembly hall.

For you there is the dawn, the sound of a mob, the long narrowing tunnel of agony, a sense of falling and falling through blood and pain, lashes and laughter. Familiar faces appear and are gone again. Familiar voices call out and fade away, until you are thrown like an animal and the butchery begins, and you hang in the blazing sun which mercifully clouds over. And, though you call and scream, even God seems no longer with you. . .

No teller of the timeless story dare go further. Of course, there is more, but we must see it through other eyes. There will be a long night. There will be a dawn of terror and glory. The world will split asunder, and death itself will die.

No wonder this week is called holy. But, above all else, there is something we must realize. It is not just a past event. It did not take place merely in a time and a geography removed from us. The interplay of faces and voices, the counterpoint of argument and emotion, the clashing of human personalities and motivations, from the courageous and sublime to the contemptible and the vicious — all this complex subtle interweaving of human thought and action exists and plays itself out eternally in human history, in contemporary affairs, and in our personal thinking and acting.

I want to share an experience, a moment at this time of year which for me was formative. In a certain city I was invited to preach on Palm Sunday in a church where I had been rector. As my wife Paula was with me, I asked if we might sit together in the congregation and I would go to the pulpit at the homily time.

So we came into church by the main door. We were handed many things — a hymn book, a prayer book, an order of service, a special notice of some sort, finally a palm. It is interesting that I had never before been handed a palm; I had handed palms to other people. We went to our seats, hands full, at times feeling as if we needed an extra hand, wondering where to put this palm. On the pew ledge? In the hymn book? In one's hand?

I listened to a voice reading. I became aware of someone entering a long-ago city. I heard shouted hosannas and saw waving palms. I looked at the palm in my hand, and I suddenly realized that it wasn't a long-ago city but the city where I stood. It was, in a timeless and dreamlike way, both. In the same way it was not "they" shouting "hosanna." It was both they and we. I knew, too, that within a week it would be they and we shouting "crucify." I realized in my waking dream that they and we would shout these praises and obscenities along the corridors of time forever. I had come to know what the palm is. When I knew this, I realized I had been told it many times as a child, as a youth, as a man.

There is a device used in story telling, especially in fantasy, fairy story, and science fiction. The hero or heroine will have certain adventures. Then they will wake from sleep and realize it was a dream. But, as they do, they see near them, in the place of waking, an object that was also in the dream. And the haunting question comes, Which is the dream; which is reality? Dream and reality become interwoven. I had come to realize what the palm is. The palm is a time machine to annihilate the gulfs which separate the illusions we call the past, the present, the future. The palm is to make them one, a single reality, an integrated vision.

So is all religious symbolism. So is the bread in the palm of the hand, the wine in the throat, the candle flame. So is the water falling on the forehead, the blending of musical tones, the cross, the crucifix, the language of prayer and praise and sacrament which reaches for time and timelessness in its images and cadences. All these are the mysterious engines of grace by which a cathedral becomes the upper room, the upper room becomes a cathedral, an altar and that long-ago table become one, a modern city becomes Jerusalem and Jerusalem a modern city. Time past and time present intersect and are fused.

The reason why it is essential for the Christian imagination to make this leap is that it brings the Christian mind and heart to an even greater mystery. We come to realize that the events by which God enters human history are not isolated in the past but are also contemporary realities. Bethlehem, Calvary, the garden tomb are not situated in an exterior geography or lost in a half-remembered past.

Consider very carefully. If Bethlehem is where God in humanity was born, if Calvary is where God in humanity died, if the garden tomb is where God in transformed humanity rises, then your vocation and mine, the quest to which our baptism calls us until the day we die, is to search for these mysteries in the patterns of human history, in the ongoing complexity of public affairs, and in our own day-by-day personal experience. When you fully realize this truth and give yourself intentionally to that quest, a simple but profound thing happens. In that moment you will exchange remembering for experience; a self in you will be born, a self in you will die, and a self will rise.

A Washing of Feet

"This day shall be for you a memorial day, and you shall keep it as a feast to the Lord; throughout your generations you shall observe it as an ordinance for ever." Exodus 12:14

For I received from the Lord what I also delivered to you, that the Lord Jesus on the night when he was betrayed took bread, and when he had given thanks, he broke it, and said, "This is my body which is for you. Do this in remembrance of me." In the same way also the cup, after supper, saying, "This cup is the new covenant in my blood. Do this, as often as you drink it, in remembrance of me." 1 Corinthians 11:23–25

Jesus, knowing that the Father had given all things into his hands, and that he had come from God and was going to God, rose from supper, laid aside his garments, and girded himself with a towel. Then he poured water into a basin, and began to wash the disciples' feet, and to wipe them with the towel with which he was girded. John 13:3–5

Running like a golden thread through all legend and tale and saga is the story of the king who walks in the guise of a servant or slave. On this night we see the king of kings among us as servant. It is Thursday. There are now less than twenty-four hours of freedom remaining to Jesus. He has already decided how the last few hours will be spent. Whatever is done on this evening must be so powerful and universal in its images that it will be inexhaustible in its meaning for generation after generation.

There would be supper. That would be normal and traditional. But there would be something more, something at once utterly simple and utterly profound. All his life since childhood he had known the story of the king's feast. He had used it himself in the last few years to try to communicate the vision of the kingdom which was so central to his whole ministry. His mother had told

him the story. She told him how a great king had decided to give
a feast. What he had remembered was the feast was boundless.
There was food and drink for all. No one was turned away. All
were accepted at the royal table. That table, more than any other
symbol, spoke of the kingdom of God. That table with its feast
was a symbol of what all human beings and every human society
dream and hope for — a world which itself is such a table, where
all human beings are at one, where there is justice in the distribu-
tion of what is available, where there is peace.

That night they gathered at a table. The atmosphere was tense.
Everyone in the room knew that events were moving to some
ghastly climax. How this would happen or why it seemed
somehow inevitable, they could not understand. Jesus had
spoken of grim possibilities in the future. They had dealt with
that in their own various ways, mainly denial. Now it was becoming more and more difficult to keep an almost unimaginable
horror from possessing all their thoughts. Jesus himself was
obviously intensely involved in every word and action of the
evening. It was as if he knew this opportunity for fellowship
would not come again. Years later they would remember this
night, every moment of it engraved on their memories.

They would remember the strangely ambiguous moment when
Judas left. Some had noticed a brief sharp interchange between
him and the Master. Only afterwards did they all know why it
resulted in Judas departing, slipping quickly from the room
without explanation. Betrayal is somehow instinctively distanced
from us all. We find it very difficult to consider such a possibility
within the circle of our own intimates. We hear of it in other lives.
In our own, we feel detached from it. That very detachment
makes betrayal terrible if its source is within the inner circle of
our lives. There is a fearful cry of agony in one of the psalms.
The singer is crying out a sense of betrayal: ''Yea, even mine own
familiar friend whom I trusted.'' Perhaps that is why there was
a puzzling lack of response to Judas leaving. The mind immediately thought of some perfectly reasonable explanation. The actuality would be too awful even to consider. After all, they had
shared everything with each other for long periods over the past
three years.

They would remember forever the moment he broke the bread
and passed it around, the cup too that followed it. There was

something reassuring about even the act itself. It seemed to bond them together for a brief moment against the darkness beyond the room. They struggled with the possible meaning of what he had said as he began the journey of the loaf and the cup around the table. They did not know what it could mean to have the bread as his body and the wine as his blood. But for some reason this simple act was desperately important to him, and he obviously wished it to become of immense significance for them. Only weeks in the future would they begin to realize the extraordinary sense in which they themselves were being called to be a body of men and women, even more mysteriously *his* body. They were not to know that, thousands of years in the future, men and women meeting in the Master's name would break the bread and drink from the cup as they had done in that room on that last Thursday night.

But, there was one more thing they would see vividly in their minds eye for the rest of their lives. At a particular point in the meal Jesus rose, took the rough towel and the water container set by the entrance, and returned to the table. Instead of sitting down he stripped as if for work and, turning to Peter, kneeled before him to wash his feet. Peter's confusion of emotions was total. Astonishment, anger, embarrassment mingled and focused in his absolute refusal to allow Jesus to touch him in that particular way. The words were terse, almost angry. ''You will never wash my feet!'' Jesus' reply was quietly but totally authoritative: ''If I do not wash you, you have no part in me.'' Simon accepted the footwashing, as did they all. The only sound in the room was the sound of the water softly splashing and trickling as his hands tended them one by one, until the task was done.

When he placed the basin and the towel aside and returned to the table, their eyes met his in the silence. He said with utmost simplicity, ''If I then, your Lord and Teacher, have washed your feet, you also ought to wash one another's feet.'' The image of our Lord bent over his task in the shadowed upper room has come down the centuries. Also down the centuries has come the never-ending clash between the teaching of that scene and the part of our human nature which makes it almost impossible for us to accept that teaching. What our Lord chose to do was typical of his instinctive genius for the piercing, unforgettable image. To wash the feet of a guest was, in that culture, the most menial of tasks.

Its action issued a devastating challenge to all human images and concepts of such things as power, authority, and leadership.

There is an echo of our Lord's example in the life of Mahatma Ghandi. In his own culture Ghandi chose the cleaning of latrines as a way to demonstrate the same truth which Jesus had taught. As with our Lord's disciples, Ghandi's friends and his wife were appalled and rebellious. Again, the simple task chosen served to teach the paradox that we all find so difficult in our lives, the paradox that ultimate power in the kingdom of God is shown in service.

That is so easy and neat and virtuous to say. It is also probably the point at which the kingdom of God, as envisioned by Jesus, comes into sharpest conflict with all our human experience. Even the disciples had the greatest difficulty accepting the reality that true power is service. They must have heard him speak about it, but there is ample evidence that they did not understand it. Or perhaps they employed the devices which have been used ever since to deal with it: they probably admired its immense idealism while continuing to ignore its practice. In other words they may, like generations after them, have used adjectives such as *naïve* and *idealistic*. They, as we do, probably used the word *"but"* a great deal about Jesus' teaching of power and servanthood. It was wonderful but . . . admirable but . . . beautiful but. . . .

Even in the room that night of the supper, they wrestled with this. They showed themselves able to miss the point utterly. It is Luke who tells us of it. He says that, even after the bread and the wine had been shared, an argument started. "A dispute," Luke says, "arose among them." About what? Luke is quite blunt. He says that it was about "which of them was to be regarded as the greatest." Jesus at some point intervenes. He shows himself totally realistic about the radical quality of what he is teaching. He acknowledges that human political and social structures are built on power and hierarchical levels. Not for a moment does he deny it. He then asks for a radical rejection of all that in the Christian community. He speaks of a "leader as one who serves."

It is not the first time this collision has come. Only days before, as they climbed up from the Jordan valley to Jerusalem, two of them, James and John, had chosen a quiet moment to approach him. Basically they made a request for power. They showed, in a single totally self-centred inquiry, that they had understood nothing of what he had tried to communicate about the nature of real power and authority. Jesus was so appalled by their bid for special status that he called all of them together. Once again he described the basis for authority and rule in the society around them. Its basis was and is power. He then implored them to realize that among them the basis for authority is servanthood.

It was probably not the first time. We know it will not be the last. We see it come up again the very last evening they are together. Again and again, as the years turn into decades and the decades to centuries, his disciples will forget those words about being the servant of all. They will choose power rather than servanthood. Within a single generation the community in Corinth — rich, sophisticated, and cosmopolitan — will forsake servanthood for selfishness. They will push for position. They will misuse the most sacred sacramental things given to them, making them instruments of vulgarity and decadence. Social position will entail a cruel struggle. So much of this reaching for position and power will go on that Paul will have to write the sternest letter of his life. He will charge them with receiving sacred things so unworthily as to be ''profaning the body and blood of the Lord.''

Paul knew that, if Christians misunderstand the meal Christ has given them, then all is lost. The meal was and is the pattern within time of God's eternal kingdom. Eucharist among the people of God is a making real within time what is eternally real in the presence of God. It is forming a community where all men and women, rich and poor, brilliant and mediocre, practical and intellectual, so-called successful or so-called unsuccessful, may for a short time be totally at one. What makes them one is their common and equal need for Christ. To realize that is to eradicate position and power and status and privilege. Kneeling at the altar reduces all to the role of servant. We should also say that kneeling at the altar, far from reducing anyone, lifts us beyond any human differences to the common glory of being the servants of our Lord!

It was the knowledge of these things which made Paul's pen fly over the parchment as he pleaded with the Christians of Corinth to recognize what Christian community was and always will be about. It will always be based on a common realization of a com-

mon need for the grace of Christ. That realization, to the degree
that it is present, is the bonding of Christians. If all have a common need of Christ, then each becomes capable of accepting the
other for what he or she is, a suppliant. Likewise, because each
of us is accepted by others, each of us is enabled to accept him
or herself as someone who, in spite of one's all too obvious
humanity, has become a living cell in the body of Christ!

There is another word we might use instead of *acceptance*. It is
the word *love*. We might say that Christian community is possible to the degree that we love one another for the common need
we have of Christ. When we do so, we are being obedient to a
command. It is easy to forget that. Our Lord gave us very few
actual commands. He told us to baptize. He told us to eat the
bread and to drink the wine. He told us one more thing. It too
took place in the room in which bread and wine were for the first
time shared, where the towel and the water were used to wash
the feet of the disciples. He said to them, ''A new commandment
I give you, that you love one another as I have loved you.'' In
a Latin version of scripture the royal plural is used for ''I command you.'' The word in Latin is *mandamus*, hence the name of
this day, the eve of Good Friday. Little wonder that the old
language used the royal *we*. He who gave us the commandment
was not only king but king of kings. Yet, being a king, he was
a servant. In the world's eye such a thing is foolishness. In the
kingdom of heaven such a thing is truth.

A Place of a Skull

He was despised and rejected by men; a man of sorrows, and acquainted with grief; and as one from whom men hide their faces he was despised, and we esteemed him not. Surely he has borne our griefs and carried our sorrows; yet we esteemed him stricken, smitten by God, and afflicted. Isaiah 53:3–4

Consequently, when Christ came into the world, he said, ''Sacrifices and offerings thou hast not desired, but a body hast thou prepared for me; in burnt offerings and sin offerings thou hast taken no pleasure. Then I said, 'Lo, I have come to do thy will, O God,' as it is written of me in the roll of the book.'' Hebrews 10:5–7

Since then we have a great high priest who has passed through the heavens, Jesus, the Son of God, let us hold fast our confession. For we have not a high priest who is unable to sympathize with our weaknesses, but one who in every respect has been tempted as we are, yet without sin. Let us then with confidence draw near to the throne of grace, that we may receive mercy and find grace to help in time of need. Hebrews 4:14–16

After this Jesus, knowing that all was now finished, said (to fulfil the scripture), ''I thirst.'' A bowl full of vinegar stood there; so they put a sponge full of the vinegar on hyssop and held it to his mouth. When Jesus had received the vinegar, he said, ''It is finished''; and he bowed his head and gave up his spirit. John 19:28–30

All across this country at this moment millions of people are preparing for a break. They are doing countless ordinary human things. Cars will be specially checked for a long drive. Extra groceries will be bought. Liquor stores will be busier than on other weekends. Movie houses will buy bigger advertisement space in

the paper. Politicians will gratefully head homeward to their con-
stituencies. People will scan weather forecasts. The pulse of all
life quickens. We begin to seek the sun and the first promise of
springtime.

Among all these activities there will be the comings and goings
of a minority. They too will do many of the things I have listed
above. But they will do them with some different priorities. While
they are doing them, these people will also be looking for
something else hidden in these days. One part of that minority
are called Jews, the others are called Christians. It is very important for us to speak of the two together for a certain reason that
is becoming clearer only in recent decades. While one of these
minorities, the Jewish, has to its great cost known well for many
centuries what it means to be a minority, the other, the Christian, is only beginning to see itself as a minority and only
beginning to be aware that this fact demands a great deal of new
thinking and adaptation.

In the next few days both of these minorities will be seeking
to find another level of meaning to each day. They will be searching each day for certain memories they share as a people. They
will be telling a story, or rather stories, among themselves. They
will try to ensure that their young people become aware of these
stories to the extent that a child can understand them. There will
be certain things done and certain words said. There will be music
and prayer and speech, perhaps even dance. There will be
seriousness and laughter, sadness and celebration. Each of these
two traditions will be recalling, in ways different yet very familiar,
a sequence of events which took place a very long time ago. One
such sequence will take memory back almost thirty-five centuries;
the other, the newer tradition, will take memory back twenty
centuries.

As we look at these traditions — both handed on across generations, both treasured by an identifiable community, both
nourishing their particular community — we find that the stories
told and the communities telling them are intertwined. We realize
also that the stories have a peculiar and awe-inspiring property.
When the story of the people immobilized and terrified on the
shore of the Red Sea is told, something unusual happens. When
the story of the prisoner writhing and bleeding on a cross out-

side the city is told, the same mysterious result occurs. Particularly
when they are told in a setting of worship, we find them to be
far more than mere memory or history. They become shattering
personal and contemporary experience.

We look then at the story we possess as Christians. Without
any apology we begin a long time ago.

At a moment in time when civilization had been brought to an
unusual level of order and peace, when it seemed at least exter-
nally that there was being experienced what some felt to be a
golden age, in such a time a small community of men and women
in a tiny country felt that they had encountered a human life of
extraordinary quality. They became convinced that the life they
had shared had been a kind of icon, a window through which
they had seen and touched nothing less than the divine power
that had created the universe.

In the fleeting thirty-six months of that encounter, they felt that
they had glimpsed a vision, a kind of being, a way of living human
life beyond ordinary experience and beyond ordinary human
society. This vision or way of life they called, as their Master had
called it, the kingdom of heaven. About this concept or vision
they realized two things. It spoke hauntingly of a lost human
quality which a person could joyfully give a whole lifetime to find.
Also it showed, painfully and brutally, that the one who per-
sonified and spoke of that kingdom, while he deeply attracted
some, fatally alienated others.

They saw other things. They saw the three most powerful institutions of their time — religion, law, and politics — join forces
to destroy this person. They saw him taken, tried, and killed.
There is ample evidence that they felt his death had ended the
intense and deeply meaningful experience shared with him. But
plainly they found they were quite wrong. They became gal-
vanized into life and action by their convictions that their Master
was alive. We might say with justification, "That may be, but
it was, after all, a long time ago." Yes, it certainly was, and Christians are in trouble if they think that simply remembering the
long-ago is sufficient to create a living contemporary Christian
community. But there is more, much more.

Whatever had been formed in that tiny long-ago community
created in turn a way of life, a way of functioning from day to
day, a way of looking at oneself and at others and at the world.
That *way* attracted others. It formed associations of people which

saw themselves forming a single network, even when it had spread over the known world. It even saw itself as the limbs and organ of a body, the body of Jesus whom they came to call Christ. That body, that living organism also called the church, has continued to exist up to this very day. You and I and millions of others are now that body. In so far as we bring our humanity to it, it is imperfect. In so far as Christ brings his risen life to it, it is holy. In today's world it is alive, real, and growing.

It would seem that, even though the events are of long-ago, they are peculiarly impervious to time. They refuse to become its prisoner. Instead they display an undiminished capacity to affect human life. The person of Jesus Christ exercises an attraction and fascination in spite of time or culture differences. The vivid, simple things he did, the incisive words he said, have never lessened their power to enter human minds and to engage either our enmity or loyalty. Whether they exasperate or excite, repel or attract, they are undeniably alive and demanding of response.

His taking a child in his arms is striking. His saying that we cannot find the kingdom of God unless we become like a little child is typical of how he addresses generation after generation. The full depth of his meaning forever eludes us, but the truth which it contains haunts us. His stark, vivid stories of everyday life show our humanity in search of itself and in search of a reality beyond itself in ways that link all time and every culture. The road by which the good Samaritan comes to our woundedness is any road in any century and in any geography.

But certain moments of Jesus' life have always possessed a unique majesty and terror. Those are the events of the last few days of his public ministry. Here we are confronted with both tragedy and glory. To read them, to picture them in our minds, to hear the voices of those days, to see the events portrayed in great art or great music, especially to act out the tragedy and the triumph in a setting of worship — this has always given men and women that particular wonder and terror and mystery which the Greeks called *katharsis* or cleansing.

It seems as if Jesus, to use Schweitzer's great image, throws himself on the great wheel of history, determined to show humanity the kingdom of love and forgiveness which lies crushed and lost within the human struggle, in all personal experience and social institutions. For us to witness this self-offering is to have our perception pierced, to be helped to see the truth of our own humanity, and to be given a glimpse of an ultimate humanity which he offers to us.

Of course, none of this would we possess had not certain people given us an extraordinary record of the events. The road to Calvary, the hill outside Jerusalem where public executions took place, has been traced in vivid images by the corporate memory of those first Christian generations. For at least a quarter of a century after the events, they recounted them to one another. They used them as response to those who inquired about that early developing Christian network. They began to share stories of an incident or a saying in Jesus' ministry. They began to weave this tradition into longer episodes. Someone we will never know gathered an anthology of Jesus' sayings. Later those who wrote the gospels used that anthology, incorporating its phrases into their own manuscripts. Finally, those gospel writers themselves fashioned four documents which, over the next two thousand years, have undergone every possible form of criticism and analysis, only to emerge with undiminished attraction and power. These men charted a response to this person from Nazareth because they were convinced that the dialogues shared with him, the relationships experienced with him, the reactions and motivations and feelings aroused, would have forever a bearing on what it means to live as a human being in any age.

Through their eyes we see unforgettably the network of human responses to Jesus. We discover also what those responses reveal about all who took part in the events.

We see the fragile faith and the pathetic efforts of that first tiny community. In them we recognize the incomprehension and uncertainty that dogs our own efforts at faith.

We see the struggle of men like Peter to retain their integrity in the face of dilemmas that had no perfect answer. Should one lie to keep one's own freedom and thus be able to continue in a situation? To this day countless men and women, some of them in the name of the same Christ, have had to make the same choice in the struggle to survive in political regimes.

We see the agony of men and women as they seek to retain their faith in the face of crippling sorrow and a sense of loss. We are not given any larger-than-life portraits of these people. We can identify with them in our own most vulnerable moments.

We see the struggle of men such as Pilate and Ciaphas, governor and high priest, to survive the complex and unbending rules of social structures which demand, above all else, the carrying out of official policy.

We see this extraordinary man of Nazareth walking majestically among them all. He is a helpless prisoner, the butt of crude jokes, the focus of physical violence. He very obviously feels the stress and pain of it all. He is totally alone in any human sense, yet he remains serene and controlled in the face of that which disintegrates the faith, courage, and integrity of all others. Jesus displays an utter trust that is far more than the stillness of trauma or resignation. That trust and serenity have ever since haunted the human imagination.

To witness and experience that is to experience and witness tragedy, the utter tragedy that human life can be. But, when we actually move through the liturgy of this season, we find another level of experience. We find that the witnessing and experiencing of the majestic self-offering of this Good Friday can pierce our perceptions of life. It can show us new horizons within ourselves and in the structures in which we live and work. To see Jesus Christ on the cross, to realize that he is no unwilling prisoner dragged to execution but rather a king offering himself for his kingdom, is to catch a glimpse of humanity as it is when fully open to the ultimate love and ineffable life of God. All this we are offered by Mary's son, the carpenter of Nazareth.

When we realize such things, not merely intellectually but spiritually, we who have witnessed a crucifixion long-ago find that we have encountered a resurrection in our own experience. That is why we can dare to call this Friday "good."

Easter

A Fire on the Lakeshore

Now after the sabbath, toward the dawn of the first day of the week, Mary Magdalene and the other Mary went to see the sepulchre. And behold, there was a great earthquake; for an angel of the Lord descended from heaven and came and rolled back the stone, and sat upon it. His appearance was like lightning, and his raiment white as snow. And for fear of him the guards trembled and became like dead men. But the angel said to the women, "Do not be afraid; for I know that you seek Jesus who was crucified. His is not here; for he has risen, as he said. Come, see the place where he lay. Then go quickly and tell his disciples that he has risen from the dead, and behold, he is going before you to Galilee; there you will see him. Lo, I have told you." So they departed quickly from the tomb with fear and great joy. Matthew 28:1–7*

So they drew near to the village to which they were going. He appeared to be going further, but they constrained him, saying, "Stay with us, for it is toward evening and the day is now far spent." So he went in to stay with them. When he was at table with them, he took the bread and blessed, and broke it, and gave it to them. And their eyes were opened and they recognized him; and he vanished out of their sight. They said to each other, "Did not our hearts burn within us while he talked to us on the road, while he opened to us the scriptures?" And they rose that same hour and returned to Jerusalem; and they found the eleven gathered together and those who were with them, who said, "The Lord has risen indeed, and has appeared to Simon!" Luke 24:28–34*

Here is the story. It has been kept very carefully. It has been handed on now for more than eighty generations. It's important to know the story because you have to make some decisions about it. The biggest decision you have to make is whether you believe it. Then, if you do, you must decide what that means for the rest of your life. Some day it will be yours to hand on to the future, perhaps to a child, perhaps to an unknown inquirer, perhaps to a friend.

By six o'clock the bodies had to be off the crosses. A little after three o'clock the prisoner on the centre cross cried out and then swooned. When the squad went over to check the three men to see if they were still alive, they found that the centre prisoner was dead. Ignoring him, they smashed the legs of the remaining two. It was brutal but essentially merciful because it hastened death.

About four o'clock, back in the city, a visitor asked for an appointment with the procurator. The visitor's name was Joseph of Arimathea, the procurator's name was Pontius Pilate. The visitor asked to be allowed to take the prisoner's body for burial. Pilate checked the army report that all were dead. He saw no reason to withhold permission.

The tomb was not far from the place of execution. Joseph and a friend named Nicodemus, a senior public figure and a member of the cabinet in the ruling administration, took the body. It was now nearly sunset and the beginning of the Sabbath. They placed it in a tiny vault cut out of the rock. They came out, rolled the heavy rounded stone down the short slope into place, and went away. As they did so, two women who had been watching from a distance moved off into the gathering dusk.

Night fell. Dawn brought the quietness of a Sabbath morning. Later that day Pilate received another delegation in his quarters in the Antonine Tower. The tower was his office and residence while in Jerusalem. The representatives of the national council asked that the tomb of the man be guarded. Pilate, tired and vaguely humiliated by the previous day's events, acidly suggested that they use their own militia, which they did. They sealed the entrance, probably lit a fire, and set the sequence of the night guard duty.

Some time in those night hours that small detachment of tough unimpressionable men was sent reeling by a disturbance. In their confused and dazed report, given later at their commander's house, there appears for the first time the mention of a figure on or near the great sealed stone.

Night passed into the first light of dawn. Quietly, slipping through the shadowed paths of the area, came the two women who had watched the previous evening. Their task (a gesture of love made by friends or family to the dead) was to put spices around the body. There hadn't been time the day before because the Sabbath had begun at six o'clock.

The two women looked into the tiny vault. They stayed there, mesmerized and shaken for a few moments, and then, throwing all stealth to the wind, they ran stumbling and gasping back into the city gate, through the still quiet narrow streets to a certain house. As they sobbed and gasped their news to the small group who were there, they again spoke of a figure. But the one thing they knew and repeated again and again was that the low stone slab inside the vault was empty.

Years later the youngest of that group recalled how he ran from the house, leaving the women to answer questions from a score of voices. Behind him came the heavy breathing of an older man who gradually fell further behind. He ran on until he could see the vault in the still early dawn, and then, suddenly fearful, he slowed to a halt. As he stood there, frozen with indecision, his companion tore past him towards the vault, stooped down, went in. Behind him the younger man looked forward, looked over the other's shoulder, and his mind exploded with the significance of what he saw. The cloths left by Joseph of Arimathea for the body, were lying empty, collapsed, flat on the slab. John never forgot that moment when his eyes searched for the body of his Master and found none.

They were never sure afterwards of the sequence of events which then began. All that day, back in the house in the city, they discussed, argued, explained, questioned, hoped, despaired. And sometime in the late evening, silently, with total simplicity, they were aware of his presence. The familiar voice and an utterly simple gesture gave them the assurance to move and respond. They touched him in various ways as friends do with those whom they love. He spoke about "shalom," and later, when they realized he was no longer there, they felt the presence of a peace as yet too new to be fully comprehended.

Later still, when some of them had already left, there was a knock. There came in two familiar faces, contorted and ablaze with news which the group already guessed. The two had been half-way between the city and the garrison community called Emmaus, staggering away into oblivion and safety after the horror of the execution two days before, when a third traveller had joined them. A long conversation as they went had attracted the stranger to them, and they suggested he stay with them a while at a roadside house. It was something the stranger did that transfixed them. He broke bread, shared wine, and then, as the significance of it began to thunder in their consciousness, he was gone. Hours later they arrived, exhausted and ecstatic, at the familiar door in the narrow city street.

After that the days stretched into weeks. And bit by bit the immensity of what had taken place became more and more obvious. They returned north to Galilee, still unsure of what they should do. Something unforgettable had ended; nobody knew what was beginning. Sometimes they even doubted their own experiences in a Jerusalem far to the south of these Galilean hills and the blue lake and the fishing villages.

It was Peter who suggested that they begin again to take up the threads of normal life. For weeks each had tried to busy himself in his own way, but none could settle to anything. There was an instinct to spend time together. After all, what they had experienced over the last few years had forged a bond that made it very difficult to lead lives entirely separate from the group.

The particular morning that Peter suggested for going out on the lake again was readily agreed to. Long afterwards John, by then an old man, recalled the moment which changed their lives. They were not far from the shore. Normally the beach would have been clearly visible, but there was a fairly thick morning mist. One of them noticed something shimmering on the shore. They realized it must be a fire lit on the shingle. Curious because of the time of day, they kept glancing towards the fire, waiting for the mist to lift for a moment. It was John whose intuition pierced the morning fog in a way that human sight could not.

At that moment a question came across the shrouded glassy surface: "Have you any fish?" Instinctively responding to the authority of the voice, they gave a ragged shout: "No!" "Cast the net on the right side of the boat," came back the direction. They did so without question as if in a daze. The daze was shattered when the water began to heave and splash around them. The commotion seemed to release their awareness. The quantity of fish, the quiet voice, the light in the dawn shadows all came together for them as a pattern. It was John's voice that rang, high and clear and young: "It is the Lord!" For a moment there was no movement. Fear, joy, disbelief, awe, tiredness all mingled to hold them. A strangled sound came from Peter's throat. In a moment he was over the side and up to his armpits in the water, breasting his way ashore.

So in the dawn they met their Lord. Once again he came among them. Once again he left them. Once again there was the hint of something more ahead, of other tasks to be accomplished. They knew not what, but they trusted. Over the next six weeks or so there was indeed more. Then gently but firmly, on a hillside under the great arch of the sky, these encounters were ended.

Such is the story we possess as Christians. The encounters ended, yet here we are, you and I, two thousand years later and ten thousand miles away, in a world totally unknown to that long-ago world of Roman spears, crosses, narrow streets, and tiny lakeside villages. So there is a question each of us has to deal with. That question is, Why are we Christians or seeking Christian faith? I know it is possible to answer that in a thousand ways. Yet none of those ways would allow you to escape from the fact that in some sense, consciously or unconsciously, you have encountered and have been encountered by Jesus of Nazareth.

If in any way you are prepared to allow some truth to that probability, then you have begun to experience the mystery which lies at the heart of the deceptively simple statement, "Jesus Christ is risen." For you too are being addressed by that mysterious figure who in that empty tomb said to those who first came searching, "He is not here. He has risen. See the place where they laid him. He is going before you to Galilee; there you will see him, as he told you."

Where do you seek him? To where does he go before you? I can't tell you that. But if you wish to, you could spend a lifetime finding out. Finally you will see him, as he told you.

Easter

The Companions of God

Now at Lystra there was a man sitting, who could not use his feet: he was a cripple from birth, who had never walked. He listened to Paul speaking; and Paul, looking intently at him and seeing that he had faith to be made well, said in a loud voice, "Stand upright on your feet." And he sprang up and walked. And when the crowds saw what Paul had done, they lifted up their voices, saying in Lycaonian, "The gods have come down to us in the likeness of men!" Barnabas they called Zeus, and Paul, because he was the chief speaker, they called Hermes. And the priest of Zeus, whose temple was in front of the city, brought oxen and garlands to the gates and wanted to offer sacrifice with the people. But when the apostles Barnabas and Paul heard of it, they tore their garments and rushed out among the multitude, crying, "Men, why are you doing this? We also are men, of like nature with you, and bring you good news, that you should turn from these vain things to a living God who made the heaven and the earth and the sea and all that is in them. Acts 14:8–15

"A new commandment I give to you, that you love one another; even as I have loved you, that you also love one another. By this all men will know that you are my disciples, if you have love for one another." John 13:34–35

"These things I have spoken to you, while I am still with you. But the Counselor, the Holy Spirit, whom the Father will send in my name, he will teach you all things." John 14:25–26

You and I are looking through eyes other than our own. We are looking through the eyes of a being who is not within the universe in any bounded or contained sense, yet can enter the universe as we know it and be aware of its myriad events. As you and I look through these unimaginable eyes, we are looking across galaxies of space and millenia of time. As we watch, far away, one of the countless jewels of planetary profusion which cascade through the infinities of space changes. On it a small pinpoint of light is extinguished. In its place is utter and unrelieved darkness. The universe waits. The being waits. In the same place, from the same infinitely distant planet, there begins to pulsate a blinding brightness. On and on it throbs. From our vantage point time has become meaningless. Only if we were standing on that far and tiny planet would we know it to be a period of weeks.

As we watch, the light, still pulsating, separates itself from the planet. It moves into the ocean of space. As it does so, countless other lights, lesser, weaker, but rapidly multiplying, begin to ignite and spread in every direction over the planet. The great concentration of light soars across the void. Speed, height, depth, size, time — all these terms are meaningless. To the being through whose eyes we look, all such things are illusion. Before us now, filling our vision, the great light blazes and pulsates. It is now become a planet of indescribable effulgence. Deliberately, mysteriously, it begins to blend with the light which blazes from the being from whom you and I gaze out.

The voice of this being, who has with us been keeping vigil from beyond the universe, speaks. The words are very simple. They are also full of awe. This being, awesome to our humanity, is in turn awed and humbled by the Light which has journeyed towards us. We hear the being say, ''You are welcome, Son of God.'' The reply comes in a voice that is at once as still as silence itself and yet as thunderous as the creation of stars. It says, ''Greetings Gabriel, archangel.'' Again the being speaks with the same majestic humility. ''Son of God, is your work on earth complete?'' The reply comes, ''No Gabriel, it only begins.'' There is a pause. ''What steps have you taken, Son of God, for the completion of your work?'' The voice replies, ''I have left on earth a community of men and women.'' There is silence, as if the archangel hesitates to dare further. Eventually the voice of Gabriel says, ''But Son of God, what if they should fail?'' The reply comes without hesitation, infinitely calm, infinitely sure. ''Then, Gabriel, there is no other way.''

What does that old and marvellous story say to us in our time? It says that one of the greatest affirmations of the Christian religion is that our humanity is the instrument of God for the formation of the future. Before we think any more about the implications of that, let us walk on to the stage of two events quoted above from holy scripture. First, the event at Lystra.

We are in a small sun-lit city up on the plateau of Asiatic Turkey. The year is about A.D. 55. Two men have just ignited a volatile crowd by a single action. They have come north from the coastal village of Perga. They have brought news of a new religion. That news has come into a hothouse of religion where a thousand cults abound as the aging system of Roman gods buckles under time and the strains of empire. This city has a memory of gods. It is said that two gods came here in the remote past. They were not recognized. Disaster followed. Today something has happened to trigger that memory of guilt and insecurity. In a public place a man has been healed. Obviously the two visitors have not come from the south. They have come from the heavens. The gods have come. The streets erupt.

For Paul and Barnabas the situation is appalling. It's the anti-thesis of everything they stand for. They yell at the crowd, finally managing to be heard. And what do we hear them say? That there are no gods in that magic sense. There is a grace and a power which uses our humanity. But there are no magic gods. The crowd disperses. A tiny seed has been sown.

The two readings from John's gospel take place about twenty years before Paul and Barnabas have that chilling experience. In each of the passages of Saint John, we are in a room. Someone is speaking to us. Every fibre of our being responds to the tension in this room. We are among the disciples of Jesus of Nazareth, and he has just given a new commandment. It is obvious that he himself is in deep distress and tension. He makes an appeal. He says, "Love one another, even as I have loved you." He elaborates that theme, all the time speaking also of leaving them. Then he begins to hand over responsibility to them. "These things have I spoken to you while I am still with you. But the Counselor, the Holy Spirit, whom the Father will send in my name, he will teach you all things."

He makes it plain here and elsewhere that things will have to be different when he is taken from them. He will speak again about this on other occasions. He will say that it is actually necessary for him to leave them. Why does he say these things?

Because these men must realize that the future he has come to initiate must be formed by them, their hands, their minds, their hearts, their integrity, their energy.

You and I detect a theme through all of these moments. It's a theme which speaks directly and clearly to the situation in which we as a generation find ourselves in the last decades of an anxious century. Look again at what we have shared. We have recalled an ancient tradition, and we have witnessed two events in the embryonic years of Christianity. In every case there is an insight made very clearly. The tradition and the sacred writings say that at the heart of the mysterious relationship between humanity and the creator of the universe there lies, not magic, but, almost unbelievably, an awe-inspiring and totally undeserved relationship!

The Bible says that it is the nature of God to have handed creation, as an undeserved gift, to one creature within the immense complex and interwoven tapestry of the creation. With that gift God has also given to our humanity the terrible gifts of freedom and responsibility. The universe, therefore, is not a theatre where a *deus ex machina* enters at key moments to re-arrange the script. Rather, if any image is sufficient to express the mystery you and I wrestle with, we might say that the author of the cosmic play creates us as characters in the play and then invites us to co-author what is to develop.

It seems to me that that is what the old tradition about our Lord and the archangel Gabriel is saying. A group of human beings is left. What if they should fail? Then there is no other way! Paul and Barnabas essentially say to the crowd that their thirst for divine interference is simply not the way God works. They seem to be saying that God impinges on human history by way of human decision, human action, even though such co-option of the human often means the frustration and perversion of the divine will. Jesus is speaking to his disciples. He seems to be implying that the future of all that he is lies in their hands. He will come to them as indwelling Spirit, but the choice whether or not to be open to that Spirit is their freedom and their responsibility. Moreover he seems to be emphasizing that they will contribute most to the future by their ability to become a loving community.

If any of what I have struggled to express is true, it means that you and I as human beings carry a great responsibility. I suspect you would agree that this is daunting and, in fact, terrifying. Yet there are two things the Bible says which are trumpet calls of hope and emancipation in the terror of human freedom and responsibility.

The Bible says that our humanity, which physically is the dust of the galaxies, is mysteriously impregnated by the image and breath of God. The Bible also says that the divine entered fully into our humanity by taking the form and reality of human flesh. There was an embracing of all that human existence offers, including its darkness, indeed, including its utter darkness which we call death. Thus we believe that God, by accepting the ultimates of our humanity, gave to our humanity a source of shining grace. The Bible does not say that our humanity is God-like. (There is also in our humanity the likeness of a demon.) But the Bible says that we can choose to be God-like. The Bible does not say that our humanity is a shining grace. It says that we can choose to act with shining grace.

These things the Bible says of all humanity, not of a particular religion. The Bible does not say that God loved Christians so much, or the Western world so much, or any particular colour or culture so much . . . The Bible says that God loved the world so much that he gave his only begotten Son.

We have spent these few minutes trying to express a single great truth about our human freedom and responsibility as co-authors with God of human history. Why may it be very important to seek that truth in this particular moment of history? Let me try to shape a very short answer. It seems to me that, precisely because we now possess the power to bring ultimate death to the world, we must be utterly clear about the fact that God has created us to bring life to the world. Because we now possess the power to end history, at least as we know it, we must be utterly clear that God has given us the capacity to be co-authors of the history of the future.

Why is it so important to consider those things? Because there is abroad in society, not least in this society, a terrible temptation to say something like the following: "Yes, we are given the image of God, but we have betrayed it. Yes, we have been given responsibility, but we have failed it. Now there is nothing left but to step back from it all and let it self-destruct at the sinful hands of those who insist on ruling the moral ambiguity and structural complexity of human affairs. There is nothing left but to step back from commitment to society, to step back from the whole ambiguous political process, to wrap ourselves around with a personal religious stance which waits for a wrathful God to destroy it all by the very weapons we have ourselves created and then to form by his divine hand a cleaner and lovelier world.'' One does not sneer at that. It is an understandable human response to ultimate threat. It is also, however, fatal. I suspect it is the ultimate demonic temptation.

On the roof of the Sistine Chapel the limp hand of Adam reaches out to be touched by the energizing hand of God. Why? Precisely because it is the hands of Adam and Eve which, in the great drama of ongoing creation, must be the stewards and agents and co-workers of that creation. If earth is to be fair, it is the hands of Adam and Eve (our human hands, for so we are named), energized by God, by which earth must be made fair. If cities are to become places of loveliness and community, then it is our hands, energized by God's grace, which must form them. If there is to be a cure for disease of our bodies, then it is our hands and minds, energized by God's grace, which must find power to touch with healing. If justice is to be done in a manifestly unjust world, then it is our minds and hands and wills, energized by grace, which must build the structures to bring justice.

To say such things is not by one iota to deny God's glory. To make such assertions, far from advocating arrogant late twentieth-century humanism, is instead to echo one of the great statements of Christian spirituality. It was Irenaeus, that spiritual giant of the second century, who said, ''The glory of God is humanity fully alive, fully human.''

Saint Thomas

A Doubt Resolved

Therefore do not throw away your confidence, which has a great reward. For you have need of endurance, so that you may do the will of God and receive what is promised. "For yet a little while, and the coming one shall come and shall not tarry; but my righteous one shall live by faith, and if he shrinks back, my soul has no pleasure in him." But we are not of those who shrink back and are destroyed, but of those who have faith and keep their souls. Hebrews 10:35–39

Now Thomas, one of the twelve, called the Twin, was not with them when Jesus came. So the other disciples told him, "We have seen the Lord." But he said to them, "Unless I see in his hands the print of the nails, and place my finger in the mark of the nails, and place my hand in his side, I will not believe." John 20:24–25

What do you do when something you have totally committed yourself to is destroyed before your eyes? What do you do when somebody to whom you have given total loyalty is suddenly smashed by powerful and faceless institutions? Above all, what do you do when your immediate reaction in the actual moment of crisis is to run like an animal and hide? In asking these questions I am talking about most of the people who had supported and followed Jesus of Nazreth for the best part of three years.

We see them on the last Thursday night in their friend's human life. They are tense, exhausted, on edge. Something is happening which is so appalling that nothing he can say or do can really get them to comprehend it all. Later they will reflect and recall and to some extent understand, but not now. They eat and drink like automatons. They listen but do not hear. The only snatches of conversation that we overhear in holy scripture from that upper room have about them an over-intensity, a sense of helpless and diffused fear and anger. It comes from knowing that something monstrous threatens but not knowing when it will appear, from what direction it will come, or what form it will take.

In the shadowed room there is a prevailing smell from the sweat of fear. There are periods of embarrassed silence. Eyes glance towards the door leading to the stone steps that go down to the street. Sometimes they engage other eyes in short searching glances, then slide furtively away again, trying to disguise what is at best incomprehension and at worst mutual mistrust — perhaps the most awful agony in this once tightly knit community. Move around the table as the figure in the centre speaks. Pause to overhear what he is saying. It is an effort at reassurance. He says, "When I go and prepare a place for you, I will come again and will take you to myself, that where I am you may be also. And you know the way where I am going."

There is silence. In that silence look at the faces. All of them wear different expressions. All of them are in their own way receiving that quiet voice they have become accustomed to. Notice one face which, even as you look, is working. What shows on it is first puzzlement, then exasperation. The silence is broken roughly, harshly. The voice rasps across the hot flickering silence, the words short, sharp, bullet-like. "We do not know where you are going! How can we know the way?" That cry of exasperation, bitten out by a man living on the edge of his nerves; his loyalty, his effort to understand, brings into history a reply which will echo from this simple room until time ends. The figure in the centre says, "I am the way, the truth, and the life." Their eyes meet. Thomas's eyes drop. In response to the serenity and the majesty of those words, there can be only silence.

In that exchange we have just met a man who comes to us across twenty centuries of sacred tradition. Yet not all the sanctity of the Bible, not all the treatments of him in icon or woodcut or stained glass window, can hide the down-to-earth honesty and humanity of Thomas.

It is only the second time we have been made aware of him. We noticed him first only a few weeks earlier. It was in Ephraim, a village a few miles north. Jesus and the group had retreated there because things had got too dangerous in Jerusalem. It was imperative to keep a low profile for a while. Suddenly word comes that a friend is desperately ill just south of Jerusalem. It is almost suicidal to emerge again. They will be within only two miles of the city. Yet Thomas is prepared to risk it. With typical blunt realism he at once expresses and disguises that loyalty. He scrambles up, steps back from the discussion, throws up his arms, and says, "Let us also go, that we may die with him." There again is that rasping exasperation. Thomas simply cannot understand the decision to go. It is to him idiotic. In spite of that he will go too. A man of blunt language, short patience, dour manner, and immense loyalty.

That was all a few weeks ago. Since then Thomas's worst fears have been realized. Everything in that impatient outburst in Ephraim has come true. They had gathered for the meal which none of them had stomach for. Six hours later he had crashed through the undergrowth on the hillside, his one instinct to get away from capture and possible torture, behind him the blaze of light where the torches surrounded the man to whom he had always felt unable to express the total devotion he felt.

Twenty-four hours later he had found out that it was over. All that Friday night they had lain low, keeping out of sight. Peter had come back to tell them the unbelievable awful facts as he knew them. All day that Saturday they had stayed there, terrified, exhausted, traumatized. Now and again they had had to emerge. They had done so carefully, either alone or in pairs, to get some news, to look for others. Then it was Sunday evening. It was typical of Thomas to volunteer to risk venturing out.

He had returned to find them in pandemonium. The excitement and emotion made them almost incoherent. What they had told him was so unbelievable that he found a wave of loathing and contempt sweeping over him. His first instinct was to see in them all the impracticality he had always criticized, their unwillingness to face facts, the ease with which they could dream impossible dreams. Didn't they realize that the one way they could now survive this tragedy was at least to have the dignity and courage and self-control to acknowledge reality?

There came the moment when the babbling stopped. They waited for his response. When it came, his anger shocked and repelled them. Everything in his tone and look lashed them like a whip. It was a cry of anguish, an appeal for sanity, an admission of magnificent humanity and honesty. The words were hammer blows punctuating an appalled silence — precise, unadorned, quintessentially Thomas. "Unless I see in his hands the print of the nails, and place my finger in the mark of the nails, and place my hand in his side, I will not believe!" It is not the statement of a man who does not wish to believe. It is that of a human being who has believed deeply and passionately, whose heart has been broken, who is determined that he will never again risk giving his allegiance to anything or anybody.

There are many like Thomas. Experience has hurt too deeply. Loyalty, devotion, even love has been too often betrayed. The church has perhaps betrayed us. Perhaps our profession, or our children, or our body and health — something, somebody, some aspect of life we thought could be totally trusted has proved to be otherwise, and it seems that God himself has betrayed us. When people come to us with what seem facile solutions and sentimental statements, we feel only cold contempt. We know the truth because we feel that we alone have experienced it. We know that love, trust, promises, faith, friendship, integrity, that all such concepts are illusions, useless, well-meaning, lovely dreams made all the more agonizing because we once passionately believed them. And now? Never again!

You and I have met Thomas. You have met him in another face and voice. Maybe you have met Thomas in your mirror.

All that was a week ago. That was last Sunday. Today you have heard that they are gathering again in that same room. You want to call, yet you don't want to join them. But you do. And to the end of your life you will remember that sudden silence. You will remember the familiar voice which addresses them all and then addresses you. You will always remember the still separating lacerations, the first signs of scarring being formed. You will remember, above all, the moment when the two of you touched and your soul was invaded by fire, a fire surpassing the deepest physical ecstasy of your life, and you heard yourself cry out of your deepest being, "My Lord, and my God!"

That's Thomas. Thomas Didymous, they called him, Thomas the Twin. We know only one more thing about him. We know that weeks later, when some of them had stumbled back north to Galilee, when they were trying to put back the pieces of their normal everyday lives, one morning they were fishing near the northwest corner of the lake. Suddenly in the fog there was a figure on the shore and a voice. There were seven of them in the boat. An hour later eight of them sat round a fire and passed from one to another the glistening charred pieces of fish. Among the hands reaching for fish were those of Thomas. The hands which passed it to him and to others were still wounded, still healing.

Thomas did not understand. There was no need to understand. What Thomas did not know was that century after century, in cultures he could not imagine, in societies not yet born, other men and women would thank God for the honesty and humanity of his struggle. Others would sit as he was now sitting, passing among themselves the food and drink which came from the hands of a God who had risked being human and had triumphed over suffering, anxiety, ambiguity, vulnerability. Those other men and women of the future would share the simple food by lakeside, in cities, in great cathedrals, in hospital wards, in homes. They would risk touching one another as a sign of the peace they longed for and in fleeting moments knew they possessed, the peace of knowing without understanding that the last word in the vocabulary of God is trust not betrayal, hope not despair, life not death.

Your name is Thomas. Your friend who wrestled life from death for you is Jesus the risen Christ. The greatest statement you will ever make is the statement made by Thomas: ''My Lord and my God.''

Ascension

An Accepting of Responsibility

He said to them, ''It is not for you to know times or seasons which the Father has fixed by his own authority. But you shall receive power when the Holy Spirit has come upon you; and you shall be my witnesses in Jerusalem and in all Judea and Samaria and to the end of the earth.'' And when he had said this, as they were looking on he was lifted up, and a cloud took him out of their sight. Acts 1:7–9

When the great French statesman Prince Talleyrand was old, he attended a large ball given for some diplomatic occasion. During the evening a message was brought to the assembled crowd. It was to the effect that Napoleon Bonaparte had died. In the silence the guests looked to Talleyrand for some words. He said merely, ''It is no longer an event. It is merely a piece of information.''

That can so easily be true of Christian proclamation. It is our Christian calling never to allow that to happen. As I understand the Christian religion, it requires of me that I regard the following facts as true.

At a certain point in history a community of men and women came into being around certain events which they believed were of paramount significance, not only for themselves but for any other man or woman who wished to acknowledge the validity of what had happened. The events were seen to take place in a life that was obviously human. Its origins lay in a small town called Nazareth in Galilee. The community knew him by a name which was familiar in their culture. His name was Jesus. Some of those who came to know him intimately met his mother. She had remained in the town where her son had grown up and where she had buried the body of her husband Joseph, a father whom their friend Jesus remembered with affection. He never spoke of Joseph, at least not so obviously that any of them later recorded it. It strikes us however, as it probably struck them, that it would have been highly unlikely that Jesus could speak of God as an intimate loving Father had he not experienced in himself that quality of loving relationship with Joseph.

Jesus of Nazareth lived human life in such a fashion that those who encountered him were first drawn to him, then captivated by him. Finally they were driven to a certain conclusion. They realized that this person somehow embodied the ultimate qualities of existence, which up to now they had believed to be qualities of God alone, totally beyond the capacity of human life.

At first they must have intuited this. That's the way we often get to know something. Those first intuitions are tentative and fragile. The disciples and their families and other friends must have become acquainted with this person from Nazareth in much the same way that we develop our relationships. There would have been occasions experienced, matters discussed, emotions tested, mistakes made, vulnerabilities discovered, affection shared, and finally a deep love realized.

These people then witnessed the betrayal and destruction of all that. If they had not been able to face it or were not in the Jerusalem area at the time, they afterwards heard about the brutal and shameful death. As you might expect, they were traumatized. They hid. They fled from the area. The community they had begun to form threatened to disintegrate.

Then something of immense and irrefutable significance took place. When we ask them what that immensity was, they reply in the kind of studiously simple and straightforward language that carries its own integrity. They tell us that, when some of them went to the tomb where others had laid the obviously dead body, that body was not there. They tell us that some of them, who had no expectation of ever again looking into his eyes or hearing his voice or, least of all, touching him, found themselves doing exactly those things.

So in that way they began what we might call the second stage or level of their relationship with him. It was of a different quality from the first stage. He was what he had been before the horror of the cross. They knew that, and they have told us about it in what they handed on to be eventually written down for us.

But they also make it quite clear that he was more, much more. They don't try to explain that. It seemed beyond explanation.

If we insist on trying to put words on it, we might say that Jesus' relationship with matter, time, and space was somehow changed. He was still very much of matter. He invited one of them to touch the ghastly holes made by the nails and the spear. He shared breakfast with them. But, while he seemed linked as we are to matter, time, and space, Jesus seemed to be using them in a way we cannot experience. He seemed no longer their prisoner, as we are. He was among his followers in Jerusalem, but among them too in Galilee. He had become, to use the deceptively simple words we know so well, the risen Christ.

But this, too, had to end. Since that long-ago community of disciples were ordinary, limited human beings, it was ended in a way which they could perceive. It is not a moment which can be explained and analysed and in that way understood. That is a late twentieth-century longing — to understand, to analyse, to explain. The moment is the event we have come to call the Ascension of our Lord. Christians have always regarded this moment as the ending of another mode of our Lord's presence among us.

But, before that stage or mode of his relationship with them came to an end, certain fundamentally important things were made clear to them. Especially they learned that all they had come to love and to expect from him would now have to be sought, discovered, and nurtured among themselves. They had been touched with his hands of flesh; they had later touched and been touched by pierced hands of transformed flesh. Now it was their hands, uplifted in praise or extended in service, which would have to become channels of his grace and healing and power. When they looked back and recalled past times, they realized that he had more than once communicated that. They came to realize, at first imperfectly, then with increasing clarity, that from this point on, from the moment of the Ascension on, they together would be the body by which his divine will would be embodied through time and history.

Did they come to that realization easily? Of course not! Christians have never realized fully the wonder of their own vocation. You and I grapple with this wonder. In one way we become blinded to it by familiarity, and yet in another way we never succeed in accepting it. This is the wonder — by the ongoing flow of time across the centuries, by way of the unbroken bridges of water, bread, wine, and word — those disciples, that small community of men, women, and children, has become us, and we have become them. There are, of course, the wounds and divisions of history which create brokeness and fragmentation among us. But, in spite of these wounds, there has been called into being what Paul termed "a single humanity," through whom Christ wills to work.

Am I very wrong in saying that our natural response to that is disbelief? We find the actuality of what each of us is, and the actuality of what the church seems to be, too flawed and stained for us to believe that we and the church can really now be the body of Christ! Can our all too obvious humanity be that body? Can our ordinariness be the repository of his divine glory? Can we be the instruments of his divine will.

Perhaps it helps to consider the reality of those men and women to whom this vocation or commission was first given on that mount of ascension. Consider the actions in the short three-year drama of our Lord's ministry. Could any group of people be more human, more pedestrian, more unpromising? In turn they would demonstrate human weakness. One would show treachery. Fear would make them all deserters. One would deny Jesus and bitterly regret it. Two of them, James and John, would display naked ambition and lust for personal advancement. Some would ask questions that showed their inability to hear the Master's words in any comprehending way.

There is a moment within the event called the Ascension when one of the evangelists shows us the pathetic brokenness of that early community even before Christ gives them their commission. The evangelist, Matthew, uses a single devastating word. We can easily miss its significance. He simply says that "the eleven disciples" made their way to the mountain.

Do you see the immense significance of that word *eleven*? The fact that they had been twelve had been very important. It linked them to the long history of Judaism. It was a shining symbol of the continuity of the people of God. But already the symbol was shattered. Already the Christian community is flawed, incomplete, wounded. One is missing. One has failed. Yet, in spite of this, the task of embodying the will and purposes and plan of their risen Lord is given to them.

What follows? It follows that the same risen Lord, risen as timely and as powerfully in our century as in the past, gives the same task and responsibility and commission to us in our brokenness and in our pathetic humanity. Perhaps there are discernible reasons why we find this hard to believe. Our twentieth-century minds find it difficult to conceive that Christ could dwell in and act through our bodies, minds, and spirits. There are many reasons for this lack of confidence in ourselves as agents of God's will for our time.

Late twentieth-century Christian faith is shaken by many things. That is not to deny that Christian faith is wrestling mightily with the contemporary human situation. But even as we do wrestle, we know we are faced with awesome threats and seemingly irresolvable issues. We know, too, that Christians are dangerously divided. However committed we may be to the issues that divide us, the fact of our division distresses us. We are also appalled at what human nature has shown itself to be capable of in this century, while still calling itself Christian. We are frightened by what our technologies have produced. We are not sure that we like what we have become. Twentieth-century humanity finds it difficult to consider some aspects of itself as desirably human, let alone regarding itself as being an instrument of God's purposes.

Yet, even in the face of all that doubt and ambivalence about ourselves, the Bible reminds us that somewhere in our humanity burns the flame, the image of God. While we are appalled that we can now turn the whole world into dust, the word of God cries out to remind us that into our very dust God has breathed his own life! Christian faith in its turn reminds us that, by the fact of our baptism, the grace of Christ energizes us if we choose to claim it. By the fact of our receiving the sacred bread and wine, each of us becomes a room in the house where Christ dwells, that house being the Christian community.

With us, as with that little group who long-ago witnessed the mysterious event we call Ascension, something simple yet immense happens. Christ accepts our lack of self-confidence in ourselves. He accepts the dark areas of our humanity. He accepts our capacity for deceit and betrayal and greed. And, having accepted us, he calls us, gives us the eternal commission to be his people, and sends us to serve him.

The Coming of Wind and Flame

When the day of Pentecost had come, they were all together in one place. And suddenly a sound came from heaven like the rush of a mighty wind, and it filled all the house where they were sitting. And there appeared to them tongues as of fire, distributed and resting on each one of them. And they were all filled with the Holy Spirit and began to speak in other tongues, as the Spirit gave them utterance. Acts 2:3-4*

Now concerning spiritual gifts, brethren, I do not want you to be uninformed. You know that when you were heathen, you were led astray to dumb idols, however you may have been moved. Therefore I want you to understand that no one speaking by the Spirit of God ever says "Jesus is cursed!" and no one can say "Jesus is Lord" except by the Holy Spirit. Now there are varieties of gifts, but of the same Spirit; and there are varieties of service, but the same Lord; and there are varieties of working, but it is the same God who inspires them all in every one. 1 Corinthians 12:1-6

On the evening of that day, the first day of the week, the doors being shut where the disciples were, for fear of the Jews, Jesus came and stood among them and said to them, "Peace be with you." When he had said this, he showed them his hands and his side. Then the disciples were glad when they saw the Lord. Jesus said to them again, "Peace be with you. As the Father has sent me, even so I send you." And when he had said this, he breathed on them, and said to them, "Receive the Holy Spirit." John 20:19-22

Israel is a small enough country that one can easily go from its southern to its northern regions in a day. For instance, one can stand in the early morning at the point where the Jordan flows into the Dead Sea; later in the day one can see the northern reaches of the river broadening out as it enters the Sea of Galilee.

Still later one can walk through the small national park that includes the tiny stream of the Baneas, one of the sources of the Jordan. It wanders through the thickly treed park, sometimes disappearing into vegetation, sometimes crossed by stepping stones. As you step across it you realize with wonder that this rivulet forms the great lake you stood by earlier in the day.

To read the opening verses of the second chapter of the Acts is to experience that sense of wonder again. As in the Baneas park walk, where one looks at a stream after having seen the lake it becomes, so we come to this passage knowing what will spread out from the seemingly small local event it describes. In fact, the real wonder for us is that we are witnessing the source from which flows the vast reality that today is Christianity.

Could one have seen that vast and varied reality if one had been in the watching, astonished crowd who saw it begin? I suspect not, anymore than we could see vast possibilities in some street disturbance or in any small group of seemingly wild enthusiasts. Given the culture we come from, we would probably feel a strong wish to move away from the area as quickly as possible and regale friends with the quaint and crazy incident we had walked into by accident!

What was it like to have been in that room on that day at that moment when something happened so vividly and so powerfully that it has no ending? It isn't as useless to try to capture that experience as one might think. There have been countless such moments since, moments when the divine energy and the human heart interlock, and there is light and fire and an uncomprehending joy. It happens to individuals and to societies, to congregations and to small groups. It happened across the life of the United States in the nineteenth century in what is always called "the great awakening." It happens to an individual in the midst of others, leaving those others unaffected. John Wesley standing among companions felt his heart "strangely warmed," and in that moment the whole future direction of his life was set. From that small beginning there spreads a renewing tide across a whole society. Human spirit and Holy Spirit interface and meld into one another.

Language fails when you try to describe this mysterious encounter. You can notice Luke searching for language as he tries to describe what took place at that first Pentecost. He is struggling probably because those who tried to describe their experience struggled to articulate it to him. So often in television today, after some awful event, an interviewer will say, ''How did you feel when such and such happened?'' The person trying to find words to express the enormity of the experience, very often will grope for simile to describe it. It was ''like'' this or ''like'' that.

So it is with this first Pentecost. They are together. That at least is clear and factual. They gather frequently during these weeks after the horror and the ecstasy, the dying and the rising, the obscene cross and the inexplicable sense of his real presence. They wait for they don't know what. They wait essentially because he told them to. They trust him. He said he would die. He did. He said he would rise. He did. He told them to wait, and so they do. In the past his appearing among them was quiet, undramatic. There would come a moment and he would be there. There would be some seemingly simple conversation, some giving of himself in grace or blessing, and then he would be gone. Now they did not know what to expect. Only days ago there had been a strong indication that that form of encountering him was over. But how else could there be an encounter. Nobody knew. They waited.

Then it happened. They didn't know in some factual cerebral sense. They did not suddenly have their questions answered. They knew only that they were surrounded and engulfed by a supreme reality which would inspire and call and energize them for the rest of their lives. Later, telling Luke, they grope for a simile in their first sentence. ''There came from the sky a noise *like* that of a strong, driving wind . . . . There appeared to them tongues *like* flames of fire.'' Then it passes, but as always, when something wonderful has been experienced and you simply must share it, there bursts from them the sounds that are searching ecstatically to express the wonder and the joy they feel. And even as they turn to one another, desperately and inarticulately sharing the Pentecostal reality they have come to know, there is the instinctive urge to move out, to break down the walls between room and street, between street and city, between city and empire. For it is the faces and the voices of furthest empire they encounter as they radiate out from the demolished prison of the room they had been in.

A final proof to them — as if they needed proof — is that the infinite variety of people they encounter in a teeming capital city understands! A few dismiss and deny, but overall it is clear that some extraordinary power has taken hold of a community which, if the memory of their leader's execution is recalled, has every reason to be in the process of demoralized disintegration. Instead, they are quite obviously in the grip of some immense excitement. Either they have all become demented and are to be pitied, or they have touched ultimate reality and are to be envied!

Twenty centuries have passed, and there are witnesses among us, men and women who know that what happened that day was not madness or illusion but utter reality. The reason we know this in our day is quite simply that the reality that comes like wind and fire, that defies our most articulate tongues to describe it, is felt in Christian experience today.

Humanly speaking, the Christian community is as fallible, as foolish, as sinful as any other human institution. There are extremely valid reasons why, logically, it should long have been swept from the stage of history. It has included self-seekers and villians, imposters and hypocrites, unworthy men and women of every conceivable type. Yet it lives, and out of its sometimes numbing ordinariness there can blaze human action so lovely and so clear of God that it leaves us almost blinded by its moral greatness. Not a century, not even a decade goes by without some spiritual giant appearing in the world-wide Christian community, often in places of contemporary crucifixion where great courage and sacrifice are demanded.

How can this be? Perhaps there is an indication in both of the readings that follow Luke's telling of the event itself.

John allows us to be present at one of the mysterious encounters which followed our Lord's resurrection. Notice, by the way, the word *together* which echoes the *together* of the Pentecostal experience. Although there are occasions of our Lord's appearing to individuals, it is significant that the majority of his appearances, especially if we look at the list of appearances Paul gives in his first letter to the community in Corinth, are in situations of community. Even when he does appear to an individual, the first direction to that person, and certainly their first instinct following the encounter, is to run to the assembled community and share the news. It is as if the context of community is almost the natural situation for the presence of our Lord.

Into the particular moment which John shares, our Lord comes. He comes to them through the barriers which we, as well as they, frequently erect in life — those of mistrust and fear. Into that situation our Lord brings his peace. He then does two other things. He commissions them with a task, then he gives them the spiritual strength to do it. The first gift of the spirit he gives is the gift he previously emphasized when he gave them a pattern of prayer. He gives the gift of being able to forgive.

In the Lord's prayer the only petition that is conditional is that about forgiving. We can only receive forgiveness if we can forgive. Our Lord's presence with his disciples now, his whole attitude towards them, is one of forgiveness and acceptance. Indeed, the disciples had much need of forgiveness. There had been self-seeking, lies, betrayal, desertion. Now, given the gift of forgiveness, they can give it to others.

What is important is that this fearful and very ordinary group of people acquire the ability to become more than ordinary because our Lord enriches them with his spirit. The phrase ''breathed on them'' emphasizes the intimacy, the immediacy of what is taking place. The very breath of life or Spirit of Christ is now shared among them, making the whole group spiritually rich with a grace that each one can draw upon in spite of limitations. The grace of the community will be a resource to each one because Christ is alive and breathing within the community. That is precisely why another name for the community is the body of Christ.

Paul, of course, is only extending this moment of gift giving when he points out that each member of the Christian community brings in response his or her own gift, whatever that may be. Paul insists that each possesses a gift. The Christian community is only now recapturing this insight. The whole practice of ordained ministry is in deep change because of the return among us of the truth in this passage. Ordained ministry is moving away from a self-defeating pattern of trying to be the source of all gifts, to becoming the enabler and liberator of everyone's gifts.

More than once, even in these few verses, Paul drives home the point that not only has every Christian a gift to give to the worshipping community, but every gift in the vast spectrum of our abilities and limitations is the creation of the Holy Spirit. There are not, then, spiritual gifts and unspiritual gifts (whatever that could mean). All gifts are spiritual because all gifts build the body of Christ and that body is the home, if you will, of the Holy Spirit.

To say that the church as the body of Christ is the house of the Holy Spirit does not mean that the Holy Spirit is a prisoner in that house! The Holy Spirit inhabits the city in which that worshipping community is. The Holy Spirit is a Spirit in streets, elevators, boardrooms, restaurants, clinics, garages, lecture rooms, hospital corridors. In whatever place a believer offers his or her gifts to Christ, there in that place the Holy Spirit is present.

We have come a long way from that first Pentecostal wind and fire. We have travelled this far precisely because the Spirit, which in that moment exercised its power dramatically and suddenly, also acts hour by hour, day by day, in you and in me, and in millions of men and women. It is sometimes dramatic and instantaneously transforming. More often it is neither. As the coming of Christ was itself deceptively simple, a disguised coming, so the coming of the Holy Spirit can be deceptively simple, a thing of quietness, a gradual growing in awareness, a sense of direction changed, a sense of deeper meaning. It can be a sense of One coming into our life and saluting us, as he did the disciples, with the word *shalom*.

A Power in Servanthood

Yet it was the will of the Lord to bruise him; he has put him to grief; when he makes himself an offering for sin, he shall see his offspring, he shall prolong his days; the will of the Lord shall prosper in his hand; he shall see the fruit of the travail of his soul and be satisfied; by his knowledge shall the righteous one, my servant, make many to be accounted righteous; and he shall bear their iniquities. Therefore I will divide him a portion with the great, and he shall divide the spoil with the strong; because he poured out his soul to death, and was numbered with the transgressors; yet he bore the sin of many, and made intercession for the transgressors. Isaiah 53:10–12

And James and John, the sons of Zebedee, came forward to him, and said to him, "Teacher, we want you to do for us whatever we ask of you." And he said to them, "What do you want me to do for you?" And they said to him, "Grant us to sit, one at your right hand and one at your left, in your glory." Mark 10:35–37

Sometimes when you and I are lucky enough to get outside the city we can look up into the night sky and see its glory. Sometimes, if we are lucky, we can see, moving across the pattern of the stars, a pinpoint of light. We know that pinpoint to be a satellite. It is one of many that circle the earth, an extension of our human sensing, watching, listening, relaying, measuring, even in a technological sense, talking. Suppose that on a summer's night in 521 B.C. such a body had moved into the skies of this planet, its technology linked to some infinitely distant source, its eyes and ears and computerized brain focused on the planet below. Would it have realized that it was about to share one of the most extraordinary moments in the development of the human spiritual journey?

Here is what that satellite would have encountered on that single night. Somewhere on the plains of northern China it would have heard a voice of a new Way. That voice came from the young Confucius, creating a philosophy which was to shape a quarter of the world.

As the silent watcher moved over the planet, crossing beyond the white majesty of the Himalayas, it would have heard another voice, a gentle voice speaking of serenity, of enlightenment. That was the voice of Siddhartha Gautama, the Buddha.

On across the planet the technological watcher goes. Poised above the high plains of Persia it would hear a singer. The song would rise high and exalted and infinitely majestic from the dark world. It would sing of one who suffered for others, who was a servant and thus greater than all kings. That voice would be the voice of Isaiah the singer, the poet, the prophet.

On even farther across the earth to a hillside in southern Greece where a mother speaks to her child. The boy is six years of age. He has not yet set foot in the city perched on a hilltop a few miles away. One day soon he will create dramas that will last as long as civilization seeks for meaning. The child's name is Aeschylus, perhaps the father of all drama.

It seems as if, in that moment of time in the sixth century B.C. some extraordinary power had decided to create incandescences of spirituality across the world, explorations into ultimate meaning so rich that, even two and a half millenia later, men and women would resonate to their power and still explore their mystery.

We return to the prophet singer, the Jewish exile in Persia, whom we call Isaiah. He is searching for an image of human existence which will adequately express the ultimate quality of human spirituality. He is really asking, What in our humanity most reflects the divine? In answer he paints a portrait for the future. It is a terrible portrait of one who suffers, one who possesses authority and power, power that willingly transforms itself into suffering servanthood, a king who becomes a slave. The concept challenges all the instincts and assumptions of our humanity and of our society to this day. Isaiah realizes this so clearly that he assumes our disbelief. "Who hath believed our report?" he cries, "and to whom has the arm of the Lord been revealed?"

You and I are called to believe that report because of one devastating reason. Six centuries after Isaiah drew his portrait of the one who suffers as a servant, that role was embodied by one who was born of woman, showed himself in all ways king of our humanity, yet gave himself in utter servanthood on a cross, and took upon himself the darkest and most shadowed side of our humanity.

Today, when we come to read the gospel, we have crossed those six centuries and are listening to that voice. We saw two of our Lord's disciples come to him with a request. Would they be given positions of power when he their leader assumed power? The moment they ask it, they reveal that they have understood nothing of what Jesus has been communicating or living out. They are caught in a value system diametrically opposite. They wish for power, for authority. They see it in terms of superimposing their will on others. We should be very aware of James and John at this moment, for their concept of authority is never far from our human wishes and instincts.

Jesus retains an icy calm. He asks them if they realize that there is a cost to power, to authority, to responsibility. He asks them if they can pay that cost. Deep inside himself our Lord must have been appalled. This is something which must be dealt with immediately, not just with these two but with the whole group of those who follow him. He takes them aside and speaks most deliberately. This must be branded indelibly on their hearts and minds if there is to be any understanding of who he is, what he embodies, what his intentions are.

> Jesus called them to him, and saith unto them, "Ye know that they which are accounted to rule over the Gentiles exercise lordship over them, and their great ones exercise authority upon them. But so shall it not be among you: but whosoever will be great among you, shall be your minister: And whosoever of you will be the chiefest, shall be servant of them all."

We need to realize the radical significance, the revolutionary quality of these words. For that little group gathered around a former village carpenter, now an itinerant preacher, authority meant only one thing, the exercise of coercive power.

Southwest in the glittering cities of the Nile delta, the hands of the ruler held life and death. East across the desert in Persia the same was true. Far beyond to the northeast the high civilization of China was based on absolute authority and constant struggle for power. West across the Mediterranean the legions of Caesar were the armoured symbols of authority. Only in the hills and valleys of Hellenic Greece was there a beginning of other possibilities of authority, exercised not as power but as moral and intellectual quality. Even that was stained by elements of slavery. Against that vast array of rules and armies surrounding them, our Lord spoke that day to the tiny group. Today we speak those words again. "Whatsoever of you will be the chiefest, shall be servant of all." In what sense do our Lord's words come to us across time from that day?

We live in a time of horribly augmented power accompanied by tragically diminished moral authority. Yet, in a strange new way, we are discovering the truth spoken by our Lord, that real power is servanthood. The way in which Christ, as the Lord of history, is saying it to us can be expressed in a single phrase: in the late twentieth century the age-old kind of power is no longer working. Power can no longer be subjugation.

Consider the following realities today. We are realizing that the economies of all nations will have to serve one another. Individual elements of the global economy can no longer wrestle for power without betraying the whole, but must become the servants of the whole.

In the human enterprise we are realizing that the technical and the philosophical, the secular and the sacred are no longer powers pushing against one another, but must serve one another if there is to be a human factor.

In the political realm the ultimate judgement on all governments is not whether they can subjugate, but whether government can be a creative servant within the complex interplay of other social forces.

In the revolution of sexual roles and sexual identity the real issue is how men and women can, in the deepest and most creative sense, serve one another. Within our individual personalities the revolution is asking how best we can make both our masculinity and femininity serve the formation of our full humanity.

Even in matters of the earth's ecology the revolutionary element of servanthood has come home in our generation. In Genesis the ancient admonition is given to subdue the earth, to subjugate nature. So it was interpreted, particularly in the last few centuries. What is the new reality? A voice has corrected that old interpretation. A voice has spoken telling us that if we wish to exercise authority over the created order, over the planet, we must do it as servants of God's creation.

The issue is one of power finding its ultimate authority in servanthood. Why can we not ignore that call? Because, as the century begins to close, the evidence of its truth is all around us. Perhaps there is an even greater reason. The exercise of ultimate servanthood by our Lord was of such power that it refused to be conquered by death. The suffering servant becomes the risen Lord. What this says to us is that power as servanthood is not an ancient religious dream in a remote and simpler past world. It is the truth at the heart of the human process which makes possible the future which God wills for us all.

A Faith in Transition

I will take my stand to watch, and station myself on the tower, and look forth to see what he will say to me, and what I will answer concerning my complaint. And the Lord answered me: "Write the vision; make it plain upon tablets, so he may run who reads it. For still the vision awaits its time; it hastens to the end — it will not lie. If it seem slow, wait for it; it will surely come, it will not delay. Behold, he whose soul is not upright in him shall fail, but the righteous shall live by his faith. Habakkuk 2:1–4*

I am reminded of your sincere faith, a faith that dwelt first in your grandmother Lois and your mother Eunice and now, I am sure, dwells in you. Hence I remind you to rekindle the gift of God that is within you through the laying on of my hands; for God did not give us a spirit of timidity but a spirit of power and love and self-control. 2 Timothy 1:5–7*

All scripture is inspired by God and profitable for teaching, for reproof, for correction, and for training in righteousness, that the man of God may be complete, equipped for every good work. 2 Timothy 3:16–17*

The apostles said to the Lord, "Increase our faith!" And the Lord said, "If you had faith as a grain of mustard seed, you could say to this sycamine tree, 'Be rooted up, and be planted in the sea,' and it would obey you." Luke 17:5–6*

And he told them a parable, to the effect that they ought always to pray and not lose heart. He said, "In a certain city there was a judge who neither feared God nor regarded man." Luke 18:1–2*

The administration lasted only two years. There was a sudden popular revolt led by some officers. It was short, efficient, and bloody. When it was over the head of state was dead. Ruling instead was his eight-year-old son, watched very carefully, of course, by the same group of officials.

Surprisingly the new regime allowed a great deal of reform. It even acted to produce a revised and rather idealistic constitution. It knew that the price of not reforming could be very high. Everything it did in the tiny country was under the shadow of an approaching contest between the two superpowers of the time. The tiny nation was desperately anxious to be left to run its own affairs. History failed to give it its wish. Within five years of the reform program, the superpowers began a decade of confrontation. Within fifteen, one had attacked and annihalated the other. Within another fifteen the tiny nation was invaded and its people enslaved.

To succeed in being totally contemporary to our ears, that scenario, taken from holy scripture, has only to change the term *king* to *head of state*, and the word *kingdom* to *nation*. It describes in twentieth-century language the short reign of Amon, the reign of his son Josiah, the discovery of the book Deuteronomy, the brutality of Assyria, its subsequent decline, the rise of Babylon, and the invasion and exiling of Judah and its people.

The sequence of events is dreadfully familiar when put in the language of today. When we hear a man cry out across the gulf of those centuries we also hear a cry that is peculiarly of our time. His name is Habakkuk. In a sense his name is also my name and your name, because what he cries is what is often wrung from us as we wrestle with today's events and today's society. "Lord," Habakkuk cries, "how long will I cry for help, and you will not hear? How long will I cry violence and you will not save? Why do you make me see wrongs and look upon trouble, destruction and violence, strife and contention? Justice never goes forth. Why?"

That agonized question leaves the lips of Habakkuk and come ricochetting down twenty-seven centuries, shrieked by unnumbered men and women until we hear our own late twentieth-century voices asking those terrible questions again. How long? Why?

The scene changes. It is now eight centuries later. We watch a letter being written, see it handed to a friend. We follow it overland to the coast, sail with it across the Adriatic and the Aegean, and watch it being opened by the hand of a young man who is carrying great responsibility and is not finding it easy.

It is about sixty years after certain shattering events which centred around a person who has become for many across the empire their Lord and their King. Sixty years have slipped away since the loveliness and the terror of the lakeside, the upper room and the terrible butchery on the hill outside Jerusalem. Since then the story has spread like wildfire. Communities have formed everywhere. At first there was the hope that it would all be a short preparation for the return of the Christ who had changed everything by conquering death itself. Now there is dawning the realization that it is going to be a long haul.

What was begun as ecstasy has now got to be formed into institution. The simplicity of discipleship has to become the complexity of community. The magnificent aphorisms of the Master have to be formed into a systematic faith. Timothy is the new generation who must do that.

In the letter he has just received there are hints that enthusiasm is slackening off. We read of Timothy being encouraged to "rekindle the gift of God" as if the fire of faith had burnt low. There is a hint of some loss of self-confidence when we hear Paul write to Timothy, "God did not give us a spirit of timidity, but a spirit of power and love and self control." Later Paul seems to be emphasizing the paramount need for a Christian community to be biblically literate, grounded in scripture. It must be the basic equipment for Christian thinking and living.

It is that most difficult of times, a time of transition from the first mysterious joy and terror of the events around Christ to the forming of a church which will enable that vision and joy to stand the test of time and history.

Again the scene changes. In the passages from Luke's gospel we are back in the days when a group of men and women walked with a solitary figure. One day they come to him, and there is a kind of desperation in them. They burst out to him the appeal, "Increase our faith!" The reply they receive is almost brutal, certainly chilling. "If you had faith as a grain of mustard seed, you could say to this sycamine tree, 'Be rooted up, and be planted in the sea,' and it would obey you."

It is as if he were saying that we have no idea of the reality of this thing called faith. We are under an illusion that we do. To possess real unassailable faith, faith that can survive the most appalling onslaughts, is to possess something so awe inspiring as to be almost incomprehensible. When we see faith of that kind, on the rare occasions when we do see it, we are humbled and awed by it. Later in their relationship, when their capacity to continue to have faith is flagging, when their ability to be faithful in prayer is weakening, Jesus does not provide any short cut. There is no magic easy way. The way of prayer must sometimes go by the road of stubborn dogged persistence. There is no other way sometimes than that "they ought always to pray and not lose heart."

Such is one way to speak about these scriptures. What do we learn by meeting Habakkuk in his time and situation? What do we learn by encountering Timothy and his situation? What do we learn by identifying for a moment with those men and women around Jesus? We know only too well what we have in common with Habakkuk is a turbulent and brutal century. Habakkuk cries out agonized questions for which mostly there are no neat answers. We know the script only too well.

But Judaism did not include this broken and at times half-coherent scroll in its scriptures merely for the resentful howling of Habakkuk. They kept it also for a single magnificent sentence. It stands like a great rock above all the infinitely varied spiritualities of the centuries. As Habakkuk shouts the timeless questions of human experience at a universe that sometimes seems empty, there comes to that tormented man an insight. It is at once appalling in its demand yet inspiring in its promise. "The righteous," he writes, "shall live by faith."

Again and again that is going to be the highest of human vocations. Again and again men and women will commit themselves to meaning in the face of seeming meaninglessness, to cosmos when all seems chaos, to the dawn when all seems midnight, to a Lord of history when everything seems to be in the hands of a Lord of darkness.

Why voice this insight today? Because to live by faith is the highest part of our Christian vocation today, both as faithful individuals and as a faithful worshipping community.

The single task of the Christian community today is to hold faith. By that I mean a faith that is capable of facing the terror of contemporary history and its threat to existence, that is capable of struggling with the unanswerable questions which humanity faces at this stage of its journey, and that at the same time is capable of affirming a divine loving creative purpose, even though that purpose cannot be fully explained in neat religious formulae.

Something of the quality of this faith can be seen in the way in which Jewish families would use the word *shalom* during the horrors of the Holocaust. Standing in lines outside the gas ovens and the crematoria, they would say to their children in farewell that single word "*shalom.*" By that infinitely rich word they were saying something like this: "My child, we are about to experience night, obscenity, agony — a meaninglessness that will assault our deepest humanity. In the face of even this, I declare to you that the universe is a unity, reality is meaningful, faith is possible, the Lord our God is one Lord. *Shalom.*"

Leave Habakkuk and that intersection of the seventh century B.C. and our twentieth century. Put on the skin of Timothy, early Christian leader. We stand today at a moment which future historians may well see as very like those years in which Timothy served his Lord. We have spoken of Timothy facing a transition from the early experience of the first Christian generations to the more complex forming of an institutional church.

Consider the last three decades in Western Christianity. Halfway through this century an age ended. We can have the illusion it did not end because stone buildings did not topple and organs did not cease to play. But a chapter of Christian history closed. An ancient coupling with Western society ended. The self-understanding of the church, its theological systems, its liturgical forms, were at best challenged and at worst dismissed as barren and unsatisfying.

Within half a decade in the nineteen-sixties, faith was dismissed as neurosis, prayer as pathetic self-delusion, sacrament as superstition, scripture as a museum of the past — lovely but irrelevant. God was declared dead. The celestial city faded into the enlightened streets of the secular city.

In the nineteen-seventies the West moved into a journey which first headed towards excess. It scaled the Himalayas for wisdom, danced to the bells of Hare Khrishna, probed the Bermuda Triangle for the irrational, fostered self-development in a frantic narcissism.

But in the nineteen-eighties something new takes place. It is not universal. Nothing is universal in the vast pluralism of today. Perhaps the only way to talk about it is to describe something that has begun to happen in one city church in my experience.

Almost daily people come in off the street. They will be of any age or income. They will frequently be young. Their tone will be tentative, questing. They will ask about the church, asking if there is a pamphlet or book which might help them "find out a bit about it." Do we not detect, in this tentative, half-apologetic return in the nineteen-eighties, something of what we feel going on in the two moments in Luke's gospel. There is an echo of the longing in the disciples request, "Increase our faith." There is the returning realization that life is a process where the things of faith are always necessary. We simply must "pray and not lose heart."

It seems to me that there is also a link between Timothy's long-ago responsibilities and ours. How do we respond to a time of spiritual homecoming and questing after a period when the flame of faith has been low?

There is a truth in certain old images. I think of the princess and the tower. Both symbolize elements in Christianity. There is always the vision of faith and the institutional form, always the poetry of it all and the scaffolding. Always we must ask how we build the tower of the church's institutional life so that it shelters and nourishes the princess of Christian faith without becoming her prison. For the glory and the tragedy of the church is to be forever poised between being the birthplace and the death-place of spirituality.

What Timothy had to learn, as we do, is this. In the hidden ways of God there is always first an event. For us that is the birth, life, death, and resurrection of our Lord. There is then the community which gathers around the event. That community shares an experience, reflects upon it, and orders its life. That reflection and action enriches the community. But gradually in this process something imperceptible is happening. The community is becoming an institution. We need to be wary of institutions. They build high walls. They become immobile and fearful and stale.

Then by the power of the Holy Spirit a new thing begins. The event happens again. In many lives and in the church there is a sense of being born again. The birth takes place in the increasing of Christian faith in many lives, in the return of prayer and Bible study, in the return of Christian concern about contemporary issues in human life and society. Is our time such a time? I think it is. Voices cry the questions of Habakkuk about a world in turmoil. Many Timothys are moving from Christian timidity to Christian "love and power and self-control." There are disciples who are finding an increase in their faith and a response to their prayers. These are things for Christian joy in this age.

Saint Michael and All Angels

The Armies of the Lord

Jacob left Beersheba, and went toward Haran. And he came to a certain place, and stayed there that night, because the sun had set. Taking one of the stones of the place, he put it under his head and lay down in that place to sleep. And he dreamed that there was a ladder set up on the earth. Genesis 28:10–12

Now war arose in heaven, Michael and his angels fighting against the dragon; and the dragon and his angels fought, but they were defeated and there was no longer any place for them in heaven. And the great dragon was thrown down, that ancient serpent, who is called the Devil and Satan, the deceiver of the whole world — he was thrown down to the earth. Revelation 12:7–9

Jesus saw Nathanael coming to him, and said of him, "Behold, an Israelite indeed, in whom is no guile!" Nathanael said to him, "How do you know me?" Jesus answered him, "Before Philip called you, when you were under the fig tree, I saw you." Nathanael answered him, "Rabbi, you are the Son of God! You are the King of Israel!" Jesus answered him, "Because I said to you, I saw you under the fig tree, do you believe? You shall see greater things than these." And he said to him, "Truly, truly, I say to you, you will see heaven opened, and the angels of God ascending and descending upon the Son of man." John 1:47–51

On at least three occasions in my life I have been encountered by an angel. The first was a figure in a dream, the second was disguised as a stocky middle-aged priest, and the third was not visible but helped me to make a decision.

The dream came when I was a child, a very sick child, considering the medical resources of those days. In the delirium of fever I found myself within a great circle of high mountains. In my memory those mountains are extraordinarily similar to a range of the Rockies among which I live today, forty-five years later. There came a light moving along the peaks of the mountains. In the dream a voice called out of the light, and somehow I was given a way out, given comfort — maybe, for all I know — given life, if that dream was coincident with the breaking of the fever.

Some years later, when I was in my upper teens and struggling with what the future might be, there came a new rector to our parish. He had a fine mind, a warm personality, and a good sense of humour. I enjoyed being in his library. He listened to the fervent opinions of youth and gently inserted reality into the pauses for breath! I enjoyed his company, respected him, and came to love him, even though by that time I had left the country and got married and had a family of my own.

Not long after I had left Ireland and come to Canada, I was back on holiday in the old country, and an opportunity arose for me to stay there. I had to make a decision. One day I was near one of the ancient seventh-century beehive-type hermitages that are all over Ireland. I crawled in through the low entrance and sat on the gravelled floor. I knew that thirteen-hundred years before me someone had meditated and prayed here. So likewise did I. In that quietness and memory and presence I was helped to make a decision.

I have spoken of personal experiences, but I have also spoken of angels. I believe that the question, Are angels real? is the wrong question. If we ask, What realities are being expressed in the Bible when it tells us of angels? I believe we are asking the right question.

Let's begin at a point which seems a long way from angels but, I believe, very much connected with them. Since human life began, there has always been a universal hunger for intermediaries to bridge what seems the vast gulf between humanity and God. In the dawn of time, and indeed to this day in some cultures, a certain river or mountain or grove of trees will be seen to possess a spirit, an entity more than human yet less than the ultimate God. That spirit will be considered reachable either by prayer or ritual, ecstatic dance or sacrifice. It may be possible to receive help or direction or even favours from this spirit. The important factor is that the spirit is reachable. The spirit mediates between the worshipper and God.

Much the same is true in the great systems of pagan religion which flourished around the Mediterranean. Divine figures abounded. There were the great gods, the lesser gods, household gods, gods of a guild or a regiment. But always the urge was to people the gulf between the human and the divine with reachable intermediate beings.

In Judaism there is, of course, the absolute insistence on the one God. But here, also, is the tradition of angels. They appear in both testaments of the Bible. Very often they are referred to as a vast host. Jacob goes to sleep in Beth-el, and he dreams. On the great ladder which joins earth to heaven, the angels ascend and descend. At the top stands God himself. Notice again how the angels fill the role of intermediary. There is a hint almost of protection, in so far as Jacob could not alone come into the presence of God.

One of our scriptures tells of the first encounters of Jesus and the disciples. Nathanael is astonished when Jesus refers to him as if he already knows him. But Jesus counters his astonishment. He promises Nathanael that the horizons of his mind will be pushed back much further than that. He will see "the angels of God ascending and descending upon the Son of man."

It is in the Revelation passage that shadows fall across the concept of angels. Great they may be, superior to mortals they may be, but they too can fall. They too can taste pride, hatred, enmity. They too can know the agony of conflict. Something very salutary is being taught in this passage. We are learning that evil is not to be underestimated. The glory that we consider the property of the great angelic figures can be twisted and redirected towards rebellion and rejection against God. Nowhere is this more magnificently shown than in the great classic English poem *Paradise Lost*, by John Milton, and in the huge bronze sculpture on the walls of Coventry Cathedral.

In *Paradise Lost* the fallen angel Satan has about him a dark magnificence. There is pride, courage, eloquence, dignity, and a tragic greatness. The same is true of the Coventry sculpture. Satan is recumbent beneath Michael the archangel. They have struggled, and to this point Michael has won. But both faces look very much alike. There is in both a power, a strength, a resilience hard to differentiate. Satan is only partially vanquished. He is fallen but not wholly prostrate. One elbow is stubbornly supporting him. The struggle is never over. What is being communicated to us is the same warning implied in Luke's description of our Lord's temptation. Luke ends the encounter by telling us that the devil "departed from him *until an opportune time.*" Within each one of us — in every relationship, institution, community, political system — the dark angel waits for another visit to us "at an opportune time." Always there is the warning to take the dark angelic power seriously, not to think that it is ever fully dealt with.

Now, before we look at the presence of angels in our Lord's life, we might consider what elements in our own lives may be the disguises under which the angelic approaches us.

We begin by taking the most common function of angels in scripture. Angels are the means by which people receive messages. Because we have certain images of angels as tall resplendent winged figures surrounded by light, we might be surprised if we could talk to people in the Bible who received a message "from an angel." Perhaps Joseph would say to us that it was the dream itself, the intuition of danger itself, which was "the angel" warning him to take his wife and child out of Bethlehem. To say that is in no way to diminish the reality of the experience.

Consider the role of angels as guardians. What elements in modern life are seen as having a "guardian" quality about them? When Freud spoke of a moral conscience or "super-ego" in our psychological make-up, was he not speaking of that which guards against darker impulses within us? When medical science shows us that around our old more animal-like brain there is a new brain or neo-cortex, are we not speaking in some sense of an element of guardianship? Can we not think of those moments of friendship, of advice, of direction and correction we have received on countless occasions as having the quality of angels?

Yet again, is it not possible to see in the great angelic figures symbols of realities that are eternal? Take, for instance, the archangel Raphael. We encounter Raphael in one of the apocryphal books of the Bible, the book called Tobit. Raphael is known as the healer of the earth. We live in an age when the wings of Raphael are spread far across the earth in the growing renewed concern for the planet. The late twentieth century is indeed Raphael's hour, if we wish to use such language.

The archangel Uriel, again named in the Apocrypha, is linked with our experience of death. In an age when there is intense concern for the dying, when there is great interest in near-death experiences, is it not reasonable to consider this era one of great activity on the part of this majestic spiritual figure, whose reality we are acknowledging but in ways that our secular minds do not link with such spiritual realities?

For our Lord, angels were an acknowledged part of normal experience. He once spoke of angels as beings who are capable of enjoying the vision of God in his presence. At all the key moments of our Lord's earthly life reference is made to angels. His birth is announced by Gabriel. As he wrestles in the desert with the many possibilities for his future ministry, his assistance is defined as that of angels. In the ghastly fear and loneliness of Gethsemane it is said that "there appeared to him an angel from heaven, strengthening him." His resurrection is witnessed by angels, so both Matthew and John tell us.

At the risk now of seeming to doubt holy scripture, I want to ask a very important question, or perhaps a number of questions. What in the life of a contemporary Christian would constitute an angelic encounter? I ask this question because it is so easy to isolate biblical experiences into a special unique sacred world, to say that angelic visits happened in a way very natural to the biblical world but not natural to the "ordinary" world we live in. It is possible to do this, but I doubt very much that it is valid. It is possible to go a little further, to say that since biblical times there may have been angelic encounters within the lives of some great saints. This may very well be true. We would be stupid to deny the possibility. But I doubt that it gets us to the really good news that is behind the concept of angels which runs all through scriptures.

To me, the glory of angels is that they are the Bible's way of telling us some immensely important things about ourselves. I want to share an insight I first heard from John Macquarrie of Oxford. Speaking of angels, he referred to the immense anxiety in this age about our place in the universe. We are spending millions to probe as far as possible into the universe. We are desperately anxious, and paradoxically slightly afraid, to discover that we are not alone. Television dramas, movies, paperbacks, scientific journals all express these themes. It is significant that most frequently these creatures, when met, are represented as of immense power (for good or evil) and immense wisdom and/or knowledge (not always the same thing). They very often appear in effulgent light and flowing robes, and possess the power to be free of spatial and temporal limitations. Does any of that sound familiar to anyone brought up in a biblical tradition? Of course it does, because what is being shown to us is endless imitations of the properties of angels as portrayed in the Bible.

The Bible has long-ago responded to our anxiety about being alone in the universe. It replies with a resounding *No!* It tries to get us to see that our human lives are lived in a vast context, unimaginably greater than visual and tangible evidence can reveal. God reveals to us the vastness of the physical universe. Within the next few years God is about to give us a present of a new telescope in space which will push back our horizons many times. But no telescope, no lens, and no transmitter can reach from the physical universe into the immense reality which surrounds and pervades and impinges upon it every moment of every day. That greater reality is the spiritual creation, the domain of God. To say that this is the domain of God is not enough. Both the physical and the spiritual are his domain.

If any of these groping words are true, then angels are the way by which we are given access to the spiritual even while we are still creatures of time and space. Yet, just as God himself took on human shape when he came among us, so I am sure that those mysterious messengers and guardians we call angels likewise take earthly shape and voice. You and I have been spoken to by angels, but we saw no resplendent figure, and no great wings lay furled in blazing light. We perhaps held a letter in our hands or a telephone to our ear, or looked across a restaurant table into someone's eyes, and we were addressed. We had a dream, or stood watching a sunset, or asked for advice, or sat by a hospital bed, or saw an expression change on a loved one's face. We experienced great fear or pain or pressure and found that somehow grace was given to survive. In all such moments we experienced what the culture and images and thought-forms of the Bible name an angel. What is of supreme importance is that we have the wisdom to give these moments the same name.

The Community in Time

After this I looked, and behold, a great multitude which no man could number, from every nation, from all tribes and peoples and tongues, standing before the throne and before the Lamb, clothed in white robes, with palm branches in their hands, and crying out with a loud voice, "Salvation belongs to our God." Revelation 7:9–10

Seeing the crowds, he went up on the mountain, and when he sat down his disciples came to him. And he opened his mouth and taught them, saying: "Blessed are the poor in spirit, for theirs is the kingdom of heaven. Blessed are those who mourn, for they shall be comforted. Blessed are the meek, for they shall inherit the earth. Matthew 5:1–5

It was a terribly difficult letter to write. It was difficult because some very harsh things had to be said. The community to which he was writing had really made a mess of something beautiful and promising. They had all sorts of gifts among them. Some of them were brilliant and sophisticated, but their sophistication had become twisted and deranged. Some were affluent, but they were becoming utterly selfish. No wonder the letter had to be harsh.

The letter was of course being written by Paul. It was going to the large cosmopolitan city of Corinth, to the growing Christian community there. It very badly needed to be sent. I mention that letter because, by using one word in his opening salutation, Paul makes us realize how much we have changed the meaning of that word in the Christian vocabulary down the centuries. It is the word *saints*.

Paul is writing to a church where almost every problem one could name is happening, where the experiment in forming Christian community seems headed for the rocks. And what does he call the people in Corinth? We would expect some harsh language. Instead, he writes that they are "the church," that they are "sanctified in Christ Jesus," and that they are "called to be saints."

When you and I use the word *saints* we mean something rather different from that motley crew in Corinth. Sometimes we mean someone who stands as a giant of spirituality in a past age. Sometimes we mean someone today whom we may or may not know, but who embodies for us what we think it is to be Christ-like. Sometimes we mean names who are no more to us than names underneath stiff, distant figures in stained-glass windows. It is so easy to forget, as one looks at saints in a stained-glass window, that the men or women behind the memory would probably laugh or cry at what the centuries have done to them!

But, to return to Corinth and Paul's letter, it is perfectly obvious that Paul takes absolutely for granted the mere fact that claiming to be a Christian means being called to be a saint. We may be bad saints or good saints, spiritual giants of sainthood or mediocre attempts at sainthood, but all of us are to some degree saints. But having said that, we still need to ask what being a saint might entail. What makes a person saintly? I suspect that being saintly is connected with handing over one's self-will to a greater will. For a Christian that means handing it over to Christ's will.

In George Bernard Shaw's play *Saint Joan* there is a moment when Joan of Arc is trying desperately to get Charles, the insipid, spineless dauphin, to show some initiative. In her exasperation she shouts at him that there is one thing he has never learned. Intrigued, he asks her what that is. Joan says, "Charlie, you have never learned that we are put on this earth not to do our own business but to do God's." I suggest that that realization is at least the beginning of being a saint.

Let's look at a dream, one of the great dreams or visions of the Bible. It says, among many other things, something more about how we might think of saints. John sees a vast crowd stretching to the horizon. Every nation is in there somewhere. A great hymn of praise is rising to God, who is enthroned before this multitude. John is informed that these are the hosts of people who have come through tribulation.

Many meanings have been taken from this dream. I wish to take a very simple one. That passage of the Bible can open the eyes of a person who is going through troubled or threatening times, who may be suffering deeply or enduring the suffering of a loved one. It can open our eyes to the simple but essential fact that our suffering is not unique. We are surrounded by a vast multitude of those who themselves have known pain and grief and stress. John's vision of that great host is saying to us that the very fact of living life, with all its varied experiences, places us in a great company. We are not alone. Others have experienced what we experience. Others are now experiencing it. In the vast community of faith which surrounds us, there is wisdom and love and support available if we choose to see ourselves as so surrounded. We are a cell in a great body called the communion of saints.

All through the Bible this theme is sounded. Again and again, in different circumstances and by the use of different images, we are shown that our lives, often felt to be solitary and therefore exposed and vulnerable, are in reality lived in the context of a community. That great community is partly seen and partly unseen, partly tangible and partly intangible. Look at some of these moments in the Bible.

In the reign of Hezekiah, Jerusalem is surrounded by foreign armies. Isaiah, a trusted friend of the king, takes him up on the ramparts of the walls and tries to get Hezekiah to see that they need not feel alone. A faithful God is on their side. Invisible armies surround the armies of their enemies. The king's ability to hold out is strengthened.

The writer of the epistle to the Hebrews begins by listing those' giants of faith who lived in the past. Then he gives us a vivid image in a single sentence. He places each of us in a vast stadium in which we are running a race. As we run, we look up to see that ''we are surrounded by a great crowd of witnesses.''

All of these Bible passages are examples of a view of human existence that speaks to and contrasts with our contemporary experience — especially in city life, where life can be felt as solitary and where it is easy to feel that nobody is concerned about us. In the face of that loneliness Christians can expect to find a fellowship of faith, a company of witnesses to our lives, whose common bond with us is that we ''look to Jesus,'' and whose common activity is that, as part of a vast company in time and eternity, we stand before the throne of God and worship. Fellowship and worship become the words of the communion of saints — *fellowship* with each other because of our common bond in Jesus as Lord, *worship* as thanksgiving and celebration because of that experience of communion and community.

Now let's turn to what is really the charter of the Christian community. It is given to us in Matthew's remembering of our Lord. A crowd gathers above the north end of the Lake of Galilee and it listens intently to the teacher from nearby Nazareth. It hears a description of what it means to live ultimately, to live at the highest moral level conceivable, to live so that human attitudes and activity reflect the blinding moral majesty of Christ himself. We call that statement the Sermon on the Mount, or the Beatitudes.

Ultimately these awe-inspiring statements are what Christian life is called to. We have only to repeat its deceptively simple short statements to realize how this charter collides with and questions the categories in which human life is lived in our world. Its values absolutely challenge those of human society. The sad fact is that they challenge most of our normal so-called Christian living.

How blest are those of a gentle spirit; they shall have the earth for their possession. So says Jesus. Our age and society tends to say, "How unfortunate are those of a gentle spirit; they shall lose out in the struggle for existence."

How blest are those who hunger and thirst to see righteousness prevail; they shall be satisfied. So says Jesus. Our society tends to say, "How admirable but unrealistic are those who hunger and thirst to see righteousness prevail; they shall be endlessly frustrated."

How blest are those whose hearts are pure; they shall see God. So says Jesus. Our society tends to say, "How naïve are those whose hearts are pure; they shall see remarkably little of anything that is going on."

How blest are the peacemakers; God shall call them his sons (and daughters). So says Jesus. Our society tends to say, "How irrelevant are the peacemakers; they shall be called unrealistic do-gooders and politically suspect subversives."

But there is a shining light somewhere in the violent collision between the Beatitudes of our Lord and the majority of our responses. It is the fact that among us come great souls whose lives shine in our world, who call from us, without any doubt or hesitation, the word *saint*. We look at their lives, and we know with devastating certainty the reality of the power of good and

the reality of the grace of God. When they are saints of our own
Christian tradition, we are aware of the power of Christ embodied
in the world of our own time.

To encounter such men or women, whether we meet them in
person or are aware of them only by our reading or from the
media, is to have our own humanity lifted and affirmed. Even
to know that one such man or woman is in the world of our time
gives us immense hope for our age and society. Because one great
saint walks among us, our own spiritual poverty is enriched. We
become capable of a richer and deeper faithfulness in ourselves.
In a word, we are *inspired*.

That beautiful and ancient word *saint* speaks to you and to me
on many levels. It names a vast community in the past and in
the present which surrounds our lives. It names spiritual giants
whose lives inspire our lives. Above all, unbelievably and
mysteriously, the title *saint* is yours and mine by virtue of our
baptism in the name of Jesus Christ. As such, it is a pearl of great
price at the heart of our lives.

The Reign of Christ

The Ways of His Coming

"For thus says the Lord God: Behold, I, I myself will search for my sheep, and will seek them out. As a shepherd seeks out his flock when some of his sheep have been scattered abroad, so will I seek out my sheep; and I will rescue them from all places where they have been scattered on a day of clouds and thick darkness. And I will bring them out from the peoples, and gather them from the countries, and will bring them into their own land; and I will feed them on the mountains of Israel, by the fountains, and in all the inhabited places of the country. I will feed them with good pasture, and upon the mountain heights of Israel shall be their pasture; there they shall lie down in good grazing land, and on fat pasture they shall feed on the mountains of Israel. I myself will be the shepherd of my sheep, and I will make them lie down, says the Lord God." Ezekial 34:11–15

But in fact Christ has been raised from the dead, the first fruits of those who have fallen asleep. For as by a man came death, by a man has come also the resurrection of the dead. For as in Adam all die, so also in Christ shall all be made alive. 1 Corinthians 15:20–22

"Then the King will say to those at his right hand, 'Come, O blessed of my Father, inherit the kingdom prepared for you from the foundation of the world; for I was hungry and you gave me food, I was thirsty and you gave me drink, I was a stranger and you welcomed me, I was naked and you clothed me, I was sick and you visited me, I was in prison and you came to me.' Then the righteous will answer him, 'Lord, when did we see thee hungry and feed thee, or thirsty and give thee drink? And when did we see thee a stranger and welcome thee, or naked and clothe thee? And when did we see thee sick or in prison and visit thee?' And the King will answer them, 'Truly, I say to you, as you did it to one of the least of these my brethren, you did it to me." Matthew 25:34–40

In the series of adventures which C.S. Lewis wrote for children, there is a country called Narnia. It is a country in which a great struggle is being waged. The prize is the country itself. On the one hand is the White Witch and on the other a great lion named Aslan.

Four human children find their way into Narnia. They become involved in its struggle. They are key factors in the struggle. During the events they and Aslan form a very deep relationship. It takes many forms and expresses many moods. They find Aslan at times friendly, helpful, protective. They learn to relax in his presence. And yet there is something about him that prevents them ever taking him for granted. Eventually they discover that Aslan can become a towering and majestic presence whom the children know they must obey and respect implicitly.

That discovery is precisely what this celebration of the reign of Christ is about. For many weeks now, in fact for a whole year, we have read scriptures which reflect on the life of our Lord. We moved through the beauty of his birth, the darkness of his suffering and death, the glory of Easter. We witnessed the presence of him risen from the dead. We stood on the mount of Ascension. We experienced the wind and fire of Pentecost. Then we spent months, week by week, working out in scriptures what it might mean to live out that quality of life. And now we are at the ending of a year of sacred time. Next week a new year of sacred time begins.

What happens then today, the last Sunday? Suddenly and vividly we are shown again the majesty of our Lord. Yes, we saw it in the great events of Bethlehem and Calvary and in the stone rolled away. But that was followed by a kind of intimacy and ease in his presence as we read the readings of the long Pentecost season. Like the children in Narnia who had begun to see Aslan as tame and friendly and useful, and who suddenly see him as royal, so we are shown this Jesus, our friend and intimate, now suddenly royal and majestic.

Disturbing? Of course, it can be very disturbing. To the children in Narnia it was disturbing. But they realized it was necessary if only because it revealed what was true. It is exactly so with us in our relationship with Jesus Christ. Before we say why this must be part of that relationship, we look back to our Lord's relationship with his disciples.

They lived in great intimacy over the three years they were together. The culture of the time made that unavoidable. Houses were small with few compartments. The boats they toiled in were small. When they travelled together, everything about each of them was known to everyone else (as anyone knows who has ever shared a camping journey). The disciples knew when Jesus was elated or depressed. They saw him pouring out energy and subsequently exhausted. They saw him in solitary prayer or speaking to crowds. They must have noticed the fragile relationship with his immediate family, who had much difficulty understanding what was happening.

But in spite of this almost claustraphobic intimacy there are incidents when it is shattered and replaced by something totally different. A seeming gulf then yawns between him and them. It is not a gulf of alienation in any sense, but it certainly is a yawning gulf of qualitative difference.

They are crossing the lake. It is night and it is stormy. He is not with them, but suddenly they are aware of him nearby. They see him walking on the heaving surface of the lake. The image is branded on their minds for the rest of their lives. He is one of them, yet there is something more.

They are again in the boat. It is only at his bidding that they are out on the water at all. They have spent the night failing to catch anything. Suddenly they are struggling with too many fish to handle. It is Peter who feels the strange undefinable gulf this time. He has an instinctive urge to grovel at the feet of this friend with whom he shared lunch and supper the day before. He suddenly realizes they are not merely related in the way that everyday intimacy suggests. There is a further factor, a mysterious factor that drags Peter to his knees and wrenches from him the words, "Depart from me, for I am a sinful man, O Lord!"

Often in his absence they must have discussed their relationship with him. He was friend, leader, advisor. He was everything another human being could be. But there was something else. There were moments when they heard it in his voice, saw it in a gesture, felt it vibrating in the air and in their bones, and rippling along their own skin.

At least three of them realized it when he took them on the long climb up Mount Tabor. Afterwards they tried to describe what they had heard and seen and felt. They succeeded only par-

tially because, after all had been said, there were still no words
for the awe felt when the familiar and the intimate and the loved
suddenly blazed with a glory that blinded the eyes and caught
the breath and brought them to their knees.

Such were the moments, and there must have been many
others, when the lakeside companion was suddenly seen to be
king, when there was the strange feeling that all the daily things
happening to them were, after all, only the outward forms of
immense and significant things being acted out on an invisible
stage as wide as the world. Such were the moments when those
long-ago men and women felt intuitively what would one day
be called the reign of Christ.

But what of us now? We cannot be them. We cannot find that
Capernaum, but only its ruins peopled with tourists searching
like us. We cannot hear his voice. We can only alight from a bus
or car on the road above the lake and listen to the warm wind
coming through the gap in the hills from the Mediterranean. We
can search for the planting of his cross, climb the marble steps
in the ancient church, touch the rock smoothed by two thousand
years of groping hands. He is, of course, in none of these places.

And yet there come moments when, if you go as pilgrim, the
ordinary suddenly blazes and you instinctively kneel in the
presence of a king. There are moments in pilgrimage when Christ
reigns in the traveller's heart. There will be a place in some ways
so ordinary as to be offensive. There will be a crowd, offers of
souvenirs. One will be perhaps tired or hot or thirsty. Then there
will be a moment when perhaps the light turns in a certain way,
a verse of scripture is remembered or overheard, the heart beats
faster, the lips form a groping prayer, and Christ is there as king,
oneself as subject.

That is to discover his reign by the way of pilgrimage. There
are other ways. There is the way of relationship, which of course
is also the way his disciples discovered him. We cannot possess
physical relationship with him. But we have the gift sometimes
of forming a relationship with someone who, we slowly discover,
shares the Christian faith with us. There comes some period,
some episode, some event, some ordeal, some challenge, when
we are made to realize how deeply this other person believes,
how fine that soul has become. There may come a moment when
merely to stand in that person's presence is to know that one is

standing by a human temple where Christ dwells, a human palace in which he reigns.

I met such a person at such a moment. There had been for her some years of active and creative ministry as a mother, wife, worshipper. There was a ministry in a large church bookstore where she used books to reach out in countless ways, always gently and sensitively, never intruding. The illness came and the years began of pain, operations, treatments, remissions, recurrences. Time and illness revealed the fine bone structure of her face. Always there was ministry, humour, faith, trust, gentle laughter. To hear her speak of prayer was to share a totally natural and unaffected experience.

We last met late at night in a hospital. I had left that city and was passing through again. She had just completed a particularly daunting treatment. Her eyes were deep pools of pain and infinite weariness. We spoke very simply and honestly. I felt a power in her that, rather than needing any pathetic help from me, was grace to both of us and beyond us. It was quite obvious that she had become an inner country whose total allegiance was to Jesus Christ. His spirit blazed from her. He reigned in her, and therefore of course, from her. By my mere telling you of her, he continues to reign through her.

You will have already thought of an equivalent relationship in your life, one in which for a moment you saw Christ reign, either in unselfishness or courage or quiet faithfulness.

But there is, too, another way for discovering the reign of Christ. Remember how we thought of the sudden blazing out of something unexpected from the seemingly ordinary. It happens to the children in Narnia when friendly Aslan assumes an unaccustomed majesty. It happens to the disciples of Jesus when the neighbourhood carpenter becomes strangely regal. It happens when a taken-for-granted friend or colleague is revealed as the vessel of a deep spirituality. There are all these ways, but there is also the way of worship.

Nothing can become more taken for granted than worship, especially organized, institutional, regular worship. Everything can become so familiar. Even if looked at with a loving eye, a sense of ordinariness or weary intimacy can set in. Magnificent language becomes the tired captive of familiar voices, all of which develop their particular idiosyncrasies. The most sacred moments can slip by, the most sacred rituals become commonplace. But then there comes a moment within an experience of liturgy when all sense of the commonplace is swept away. The familiar becomes powerful, piercing, vivid, unforgettable. There is a deep sense of Presence, a sense of the passing by of One who is infinitely beyond us yet utterly near us. Thus we learn in worship of a Christ whose reign suddenly blazes into our clouded awareness.

Our scriptures today express other ways in which the supremacy of Christ is perceived by a Christian. Ezekiel speaks of a situation which can be paralleled many times in history. As a prophet he sees his people as having been betrayed by their spiritual leaders. He speaks of God's decision to exercise leadership over and above such leaders. Time and time again in history religious leadership has betrayed its own vocation. Fear, greed, many motives have been involved. But there has come into the life of God's people a spiritual tide flowing not from human traditional leadership but from sources of grace, which seem newly formed by the Holy Spirit's action. We see in history a display of new energy and new spirituality which shows who really reigns!

As Paul writes to Corinth, we hear him defining the reign of Christ in terms of his victory over death. For Paul, as for all of us, death is the one thing that seems to reign over all of life. Yet for the Christian there is one person who reigns even over the dark Lord of death. For those early Christians and for all subsequent generations, this is the ultimate definition of the reign of Christ. He reigns as he is risen.

Matthew's expression for the reign of Christ is in terms of justice, sharing, self-giving. Where these are found in society or in relationships, there Christ reigns. Where they are not present, something else has real authority. Usually it will be some form of human self-will. In personal terms it will emerge as self-centredness, in social terms, as oppression.

We have shared ways in which it is possible to experience Christ as king. When any of these ways becomes the road by which Jesus Christ reaches us, then certain things happen. We cease to think of Jesus Christ as merely — heaven forbid — nice, comforting, personally therapeutic! We cease to regard Jesus Christ merely as a religious symbol to be used as a personal resource at times of our choosing. We cease to think of Jesus Christ as a tradition, a religious system, a piece of history. We cease to think of Jesus Christ as a religious resource which we control. Instead we experience power and grace and presence. We experience immediacy and energy and demand. We learn that it is not we who are in control of him but he of us. Perhaps the greatest mystery of all is that the power of Jesus Christ is so secure, so loving, so ultimate, that it will never coerce our human will. It will show itself with such authority and attractiveness that our self-will, seeing itself for what it is, will choose the will of Christ. In that moment of our choosing, he reigns.